HNC HND BUSINESS

Mandatory Unit 5:

Common Law I

Course Book

In this June 2004 first edition

- full and comprehensive coverage of the revised Edexcel Guidelines, effective from September 2004

- activities, examples and quizzes

- practical illustrations

- practice assignments

- glossary of terms and index

EDEXCEL HNC & HND BUSINESS

First edition June 2004

ISBN 07517 1247 7

British Library Cataloguing-in Publication Data

A catalogue record for this book is available from the British Library

Printed in Great Britain by W M Print

45-47 Frederick Street

Walsall, West Midlands

WS2 9NE

Published by

BPP Professional Education

Aldine House, Aldine Place

London W12 8AW

www.bpp.com

We are grateful to Edexcel for permission to reproduce the Guidelines in
this text.

CONTENTS

INTRODUCTION

Edexcel has revised the structure of the HND/HNC qualifications in Business, and its Guidelines covering the content of each Unit. These changes are effective from September 2004. This book has been **written specifically to cover the revised Guidelines** and provides concise yet comprehensive coverage.

The HNC and HND qualifications in Business have always been very demanding. The suggested content, set out by Edexcel in Guidelines for each unit, includes topics which are normally covered at degree level. Students therefore need books which get straight to the core of these topics, and which build upon the student's existing knowledge and experience. BPP's series of Course Books have been designed to meet that need.

This book has been written specifically for Unit 5: *Common Law I*. It covers the Edexcel guidelines and suggested content in full, and includes the following features.

- The Edexcel guidelines

- A study guide explaining the key features of the book and how to get the most from your studies

- A glossary and index

- Assignments

Each chapter contains:

- An introduction and study objectives

- Summary diagrams and signposts, to guide you through the chapter

- Numerous activities, topics for discussion, definitions and examples, all designed to bring the subject to life and enable students to apply their learning to practical situations

- A chapter roundup, a quick quiz with answers and answers to activities

BPP Professional Education are the leading providers of targeted texts for professional qualifications. Our customers need to study effectively. They cannot afford to waste time. They expect clear, concise and highly-focused study material. This series of Course Books for HNC and HND Business has been designed and produced to fulfil those needs.

BPP Professional Education
2004

Other titles in this series:
Mandatory units

Unit 1	Marketing
Unit 2	Managing Financial Resources and Decisions
Unit 3	Organisations and Behaviour
Unit 4	Business Environment
Unit 5	Common Law 1
Unit 6	Business Decision Making
Unit 7	Business Strategy
Unit 8	Research Project

Endorsed title routes

Units 9-12	Finance
Units 13-16	Management
Units 17-20	Marketing
Units 21-24	Human Resource Management
Units 25-28	Law

For more information, or to place an order, please call 020 8740 2211, or fill in the order form at the back of this book.

If you would like to send in your comments on this book, please turn to the review form on the last page.

EDEXCEL GUIDELINES FOR MANDATORY UNIT 5: COMMON LAW I

Description of unit

The aim of this unit is to provide an introduction to the law of contract, with a particular focus on the formation and operation of a business contract. Learners are encouraged to explore the contents of such an agreement and, in particular, to appreciate the practical application of standard-form business contracts. Additionally, the unit enables learners to understand how the Law of Tort differs from the law of contract and examines the Tort of Negligence and issues of liability pertinent to business.

Summary of learning outcomes

To achieve this unit a student must:

1. Understand the **essential elements of a valid** and legally binding **contract** and its role in a business context.

2. Explore the significance of **specific terms in a business contract**

3. Examine the role of the **Law of Tort in business activities** assessing **particular forms of tortious liability**

4. Understand and apply the **elements of the Tort of Negligence**

Content	Covered in chapter(s)
1 Essential elements of a valid contract	
Essential elements: types of contractual agreements and their application in business: the making of a valid offer and its unconditional acceptance; the essential existence of a clear and unambiguous intention supported by sufficient consideration; the parties to the agreement possessing the necessary capacity and being privy to the agreement.	3–6
2 Specific terms in a business contract	
Specific terms: contents of a valid agreement, and standard form business contracts; comparative analysis of express and implied terms; the effects of the breach of a condition, warranty or an innominate term; the legal effect on the agreement of the incorporation of an exemption clause.	7
3 The Law of Tort in business activities and particular forms of tortious liability	
The Law of Tort: fundamental aspects of tort; tortious liability and business operations; advantages of using tortious as opposed to contractual remedies	8
Types of tortious liability: the tortious liability of occupiers, employer's liability including vicarious liability for employees, health and safety issues, strict liability, difficulties of practical application	8
4 Elements of the Tort of Negligence	
Negligence: the nature and scope of the duty of care and the standard of care; breach of duty, issues of causation and remoteness of damage	9

Outcomes and assessment criteria

Outcomes	Assessment criteria for pass **To achieve each outcome a learner must demonstrate the ability to:**
1 Understand the **essential elements of a valid** and legally binding **contract** and its role in a business context	• Explain the different types of business agreement and the importance of the key elements required for the formation of a valid contract • Apply the rules of offer and acceptance in a given scenario, also considering any impact of new technology • Assess the importance of the rules of intention and consideration of the parties to the agreement • Explain the importance of the contracting parties having the appropriate legal capacity to enter into a binding agreement
2 Analyse the significance of **specific terms in a business contract**	• Analyse specific contract terms with reference to their importance and impact if these terms are broken • Apply and analyse the law on standard form contracts • Discuss the effect of exemption clauses in attempting to exclude contractual liability
3 Examine the role of the **Law of Tort in business activities** assessing **particular forms of tortious liability**	• Describe the nature of general tortious liability comparing and contrasting to contractual liability • Explain the liability applicable to an occupier of premises • Discuss the nature of employer's liability with reference to vicarious liability and health and safety implications • Distinguish strict liability from general tortious liability
4 Understand and apply **the elements of the Tort of Negligence**	• Explain and understand the application of the elements of the Tort of Negligence • Analyse the practical applications of particular elements of the tort of negligence

NOTES

Delivery

This unit can be delivered in a variety of ways. Group work and other active methods of learning can be employed to enhance learners' experience and promote the required understanding. The use of case studies and specimen documentation is to be particularly encouraged, both as a means of assessment and as part of the normal learning process.

Assessment

Evidence of outcomes may be in the form of:

- case studies to assess differing approaches to contractual liability

- group work, presentations, and role plays used critically, to examine the essential elements of a valid contract

- case studies to assess differing approaches to tortious liability

- group work to examine critically particular elements of negligence

- group role play to simulate situations where various forms of tortious liability apply

Links

This unit provides for the development of a solid understanding of the essential requirements of a valid business contract. This will be a foundation for *Unit 27: Common Law II* where the knowledge base and understanding gained will be further developed and enhanced. To a lesser extent there will be some common ground between the contents of this unit and *Unit 25: English Legal System* in relation to the forms of liability and the development of common law and equitable remedies.

This unit offers opportunities for developing common skills in managing tasks and solving problems, communicating, working with and relating to others.

Support materials

Textbooks

Sufficient library resources should be available to enable learners to achieve this unit. Particularly relevant texts are:

- Atiyah, P. S. *Introduction to the Law of Contract* (Clarendon Press, June 1995) ISBN 0198259530

- Beale, Bishop and Furmston, *Contract – Cases and Materials* (Butterworth, October 2001) ISBN 0406 92404X

- Cheshire, Fifoot and Furmston, *Law of Contract* (Butterworth, October 2001) ISBN 0406930589

- Cooke, J. *Law of Tort* (Prentice Hall, May 1997) ISBN 0273627104

- Elliott and Quinn, *Contract Law* (Longman, December 2002) ISBN 0582473306

- Elliott and Quinn, *Tort Law* (Longman, July 1997) ISBN 058243811X

NOTES

- Harvey and Marston, *Cases and Commentary on TORT* (Prentice Hall, 2004) 5th edition ISBN 0406971382

- Hodgson, J. and Lewthwaite, J. *Law of Torts* (Blackstone, October 2001) ISBN 1841742759

- Jones, M. *Textbook on Torts* (Oxford University, August 2002) ISBN 0199255334

- Pannett, A. *Law of Torts* (Prentice Hall, March 1997) ISBN 0712110704

- Treitel, G. *Law of Contract* (Sweet & Maxwell, June 2003) ISBN 042178850X

- Young, M. *Cases and Commentary in Contract Law* (Prentice Hall, June 1997) ISBN 0273 625705

Journals

- *Law Society Gazette*

- *New Law Journal*

BPP

PROFESSIONAL EDUCATION

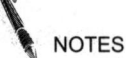
NOTES

STUDY GUIDE

This course book gives full coverage of the revised Edexcel guidelines. This course book also includes features designed specifically to make learning effective and efficient.

(a)   Each chapter begins with a summary diagram which maps out the areas covered by the chapter. There are detailed summary diagrams at the start of each main section of the chapter. You can use the diagrams during revision as a basis for your notes.

(b)   After the main summary diagram there is an introduction, which sets the chapter in context. This is followed by learning objectives, which show you what you will learn as you work through the chapter.

(c)   Throughout the course book, there are special aids to learning. These are indicated by symbols in the margin,

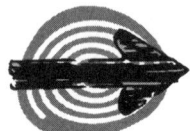

Signposts guide you through the course book, showing how each section connects with the next.

Definitions give the meanings of key terms. The **glossary** at the end of the course book summarises these.

Activities help you to test how much you have learnt. An indication of the time you should take on each is given. Answers are given at the end of each chapter.

Topics for discussion are for use in seminars. They give you a chance to share your views with your fellow students. They allow you to highlight holes in your knowledge and to see how others understand concepts. If you have time, try 'teaching' someone the concepts you have learnt in a session. This helps you to remember key points and answering their questions will consolidate your knowledge.

Examples relate what you have learnt to the outside world. Try to think up your own examples as you work through the course book.

Chapter roundups present the key information from the chapter in a concise format. Useful for revision.

PROFESSIONAL EDUCATION

(d)   The wide **margin** on each page is for your notes. You will get the best out of this book if you interact with it. Write down your thoughts and ideas. Record examples, question theories, add references to other pages in the book and rephrase key points in your own words.

(e)   At the end of each chapter, there is a **chapter roundup**, a **quick quiz** with answers and an **assignment**. Use these to revise and consolidate your knowledge. The chapter roundup summarises the chapter. The quick quiz tests what you have learnt (the answers often refer you back to the chapter so you can look over subjects again). The assignment (with a time guide) allows you to put your knowledge into practice. Answer guidelines for the assignments are at the end of the text.

(f)   At the end of the course book, there is a **glossary of key terms** and an **index**.

BACKGROUND:

INTRODUCTION TO ENGLISH LAW

Chapter 1 :
INTRODUCTION TO THE LAW

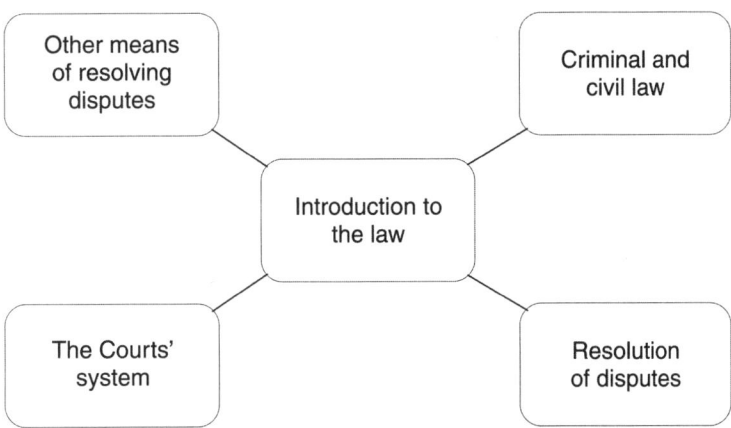

Introduction

A quick look at the syllabus and outcomes for this Unit will show you that the main elements are the various types of contract and the problems which can arise with them, and some basic aspects of the law of tort. However, in order fully to understand those topics it is vital that you have an appreciation of the background to the English legal system and are familiar with the terminology used. This means that when you come to study the fine detail of the law in later chapters of this book you will be able to put into context the legal rules and decisions which you encounter.

Your objectives

In this chapter you will learn about the following.

(a)   The role of law within society

(b)   The difference between civil and criminal law

(c)   How disputes may be resolved by the courts, by tribunals and by arbitration

You should appreciate that the first two chapters of this book are for background reading, and the subject matter would not be covered in the assignments that you are expected to sit as part of your course. It is important, however, that you understand the legal background underpinning the law you will cover later.

Additionally, the subject matter covered here features in Unit 25 of the law endorsed title route. Should you decide to pursue that route, you will find the topics covered here very relevant.

1   CRIMINAL AND CIVIL LAW

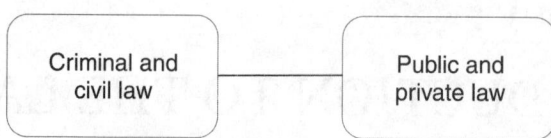

Law can be summarised as a body of rules for the guidance of human conduct, imposed upon and enforced among the members of a particular state in order to enable the state to function. If there is no legal system it is likely that chaos will ensue, as can sometimes be seen in countries where civil war causes the system of law and order to be abused and ultimately to break down.

We are all subject to the law. Its consequences affect us all on a daily basis, whether we are buying a house, buying goods in a shop (ie entering a consumer contract), entering a contract of employment or driving a car. It is not only individuals who are subject to the law: the different types of law, much of which is specific to them, also govern companies and other business units.

The law is not static but changes and develops, reflecting the values and institutions of each era. Any study of English law as it now is (for the time being) requires a brief explanation of the process of historical development which has made it what it is, which we shall give in these two background chapters.

Although English law has many features which are common to other national legal systems, it also has some distinctive features of its own. It differs from the law of many Western European countries (and also Scotland) in having absorbed only a small amount of Roman law. Secondly, English law is case law made by decisions of the courts to a much greater extent than the law of many other countries. We shall look at the rules applied to case law in Chapter 2.

1.1   Public and private law

One basic division of law is between public and private.

Public law governs relations between an individual citizen and the state. Examples include:

(a)   The criminal law, which will be discussed in greater detail shortly

(b)   Constitutional law, which is the law governing matters such as the operation of Parliament and the frequency with which general elections must be held

(c)   Administrative law

Private law, which is also known as **civil law**, is the law governing relations between citizens themselves. Examples include:

(a)   The law of contract, which you will cover in some depth later in this book

(b)   The law of tort, which is the law covering the legal duty of people towards each other, such as the law of negligence. This is also covered later in this book.

   (c)   The law of trusts, dealing with the disposal of a person's property according to their wishes

   (d)   Property law, that is the rules on the buying, selling and holding of property and

   (e)   Family law, concerned with issues such as divorce, custody of children and wards of court.

1.2   Civil and criminal law

The distinction between criminal and civil liability is central to the legal system and to the way in which the court system is structured. The objectives of each category of the law, although closely connected, are different.

A **crime** is conduct prohibited by the law. The **State** (in the form of the Crown Prosecution Service) is the usual prosecutor in a criminal case because it is the community as a whole which suffers as a result of the law being broken. However, private individuals may also prosecute (although this is rare). Persons guilty of crimes are **punished by fines or imprisonment**.

In a criminal trial, the **burden of proof** to convict the accused rests with the prosecution, which must prove its case **beyond reasonable doubt**. A criminal case might be referred to as *R v Shipman 2000*. The prosecution is brought in the name of the Crown (R signifying Regina, or the Queen). Shipman is the name of the accused or defendant.

Civil law exists to **regulate disputes** over the rights and obligations of persons dealing with each other. The State has no role in a dispute over, for instance, a breach of contract. It is up to the persons involved to settle the matter in the courts if they so wish. The general purpose of such a course of action is to impose a settlement, sometimes using financial **compensation** in the form of the legal remedy of damages, sometimes using **equitable remedies** such as injunctions or other orders. There is no concept of punishment; it is more a case of righting a wrong.

For example, the civil law can deal with matters as major as the ownership of a fleet of tankers, in a multi-million pound case lasting for months, or as seemingly minor as the height of a hedge between neighbours.

In civil proceedings, the case must be proved on the **balance of probability**. The party bearing the burden of proof is not required to produce absolute proof, nor prove the issue beyond reasonable doubt. He must convince the court that it is more probable than not that his assertions are true.

Terminology is different from that in criminal cases; the claimant sues the defendant, and the burden of proof may shift between the two.

The main areas of civil liability for this syllabus is **contract** between persons.

Definition

> **Standard of proof**: the extent to which the court must be satisfied by the evidence presented.

NOTES

Activity 1 **(5 mins)**

Why do you think that the standard of proof in criminal trials does not have to be beyond *all* doubt?

Activity 2 **(5 mins)**

While driving, Martin exceeded the speed limit and crashed into the wall of Andrew's house, causing damage worth £5,000. What legal actions, either criminal or civil, may arise as a result of his actions?

---

2 RESOLUTION OF DISPUTES

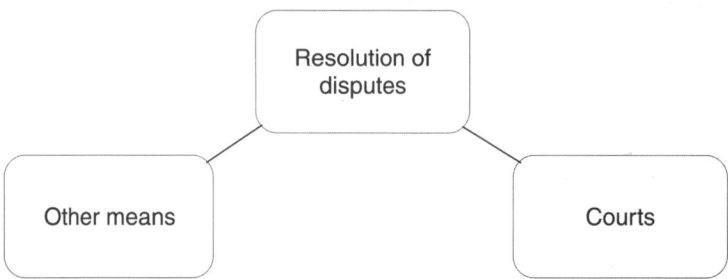

Most people think that legal disputes are resolved purely by going to court. It is true that there is a well-established hierarchy of courts, the precise structure of which depends on whether the matter is dealt with under civil or criminal procedures, but other means of resolving disputes are becoming increasingly popular. The use of tribunals and arbitration is often seen as quicker, cheaper and more focused than the traditional routes through the Courts, although recent reforms to the conduct of civil proceedings have helped to streamline the procedure.

3 THE COURTS' SYSTEM

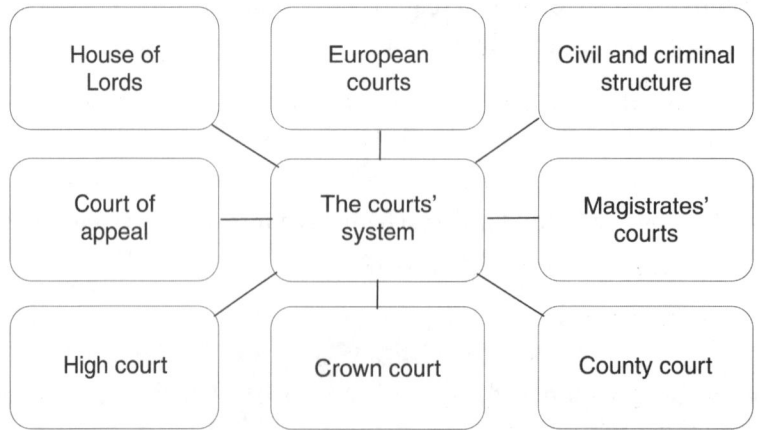

The diagrams on the next page set out the basic structure of the courts. The structure is different for criminal and civil cases, although as you can see from the diagrams, some of

the courts have both criminal and civil jurisdiction. The courts are discussed in more detail below.

3.1 Civil structure

The diagram below sets out the English **civil court structure.** This applies to cases arising in contract and tort, the two areas of law covered in this unit. It is worth your having a basic understanding of how such cases are handled.

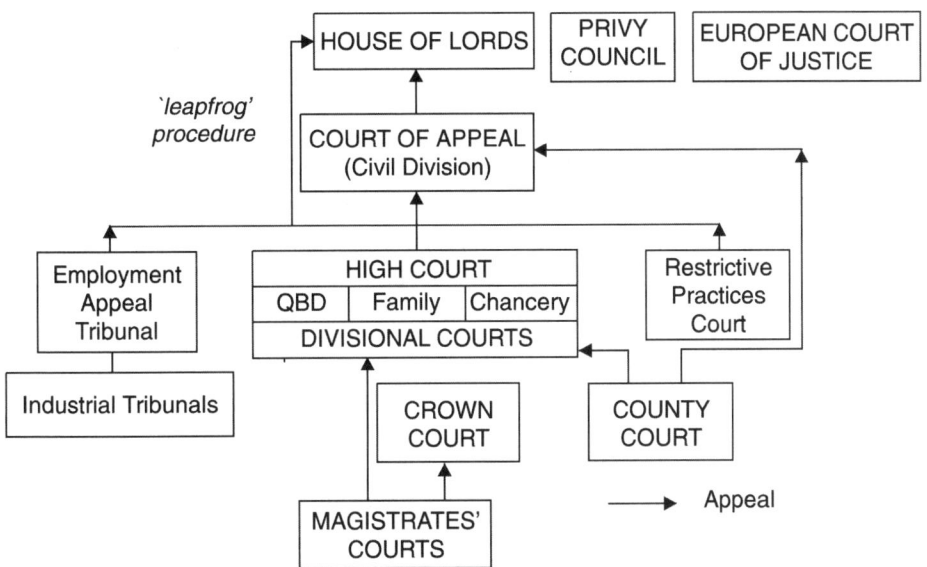

3.2 The county court

Jurisdiction

County courts have **civil jurisdiction** only but deal with almost every kind of civil case. The practical importance of the county courts is that they deal with **the majority of the country's civil litigation.**

The county court is involved in:

(a) **Contract and tort** claims, so the areas of law covered in this book

(b) **Equitable matters** concerning trusts, mortgages and partnership dissolution up to £30,000, unless the parties waive the limit

(c) Disputes concerning land where the capital value of the land is less than £30,000

(d) **Undefended matrimonial cases**

(e) **Probate matters** (disputes over the terms of a will) where the estate of the deceased is estimated to be less than £30,000

(f) **Miscellaneous matters** conferred by various statutes, for example the Consumer Credit Act 1974 (no limit on jurisdiction)

(g) Some **bankruptcy,** company winding-up and admiralty cases

(h) 'Small claims' of up to £5,000

Actions in contract and tort worth **less than £25,000** must normally be tried in a **county court** and those worth **£50,000 or more** must normally be tried in the **High Court**, with those in between going either way, depending on the case itself and the importance of the law attached to it.

The small claims procedure

To assist litigants who decide to conduct their case in person the county court registrar may, if the amount involved **does not exceed £5,000** or if the parties agree, refer a case to an arbitrator to hear and decide informally under the small claims procedure.

(a) The arbitrator is usually the district judge himself but may be another person chosen by the parties. The arbitrator's award is recorded as a county court judgement.

(b) This is a cheaper and quicker way of settling small claims in an informal atmosphere.

(c) Personal injury claims, claims for possession of land, housing disrepair claims and harassment claims may be dealt with by the small claims procedure only if they fall below £1,000.

FOR DISCUSSION

In 1996 a survey by the National Audit Office found that although 94 per cent of claimants in the Small Claims Court obtained judgement in their favour, only 54% recovered all or part of their claim and 36% recovered nothing.

Appeals

From the county court there is a right of appeal direct to the Civil Division of the Court of Appeal. In bankruptcy cases an appeal goes to the Chancery Division of the High Court.

Staffing

A **circuit judge** presides, being a barrister of at least ten years' standing. A **recorder** is a solicitor or barrister of at least ten years' standing and may be appointed as a circuit judge after three years' experience as a recorder. A **district judge**, who must be a solicitor or barrister of at least seven years' standing, assists the circuit judge.

Activity 3 (10 mins)

Penny sues Desmond for breach of contract, asking for and obtaining damages of £10,000. In which court would this case be heard? Suppose the sum involved was £3,000. Would that make any difference to your answer?

The Woolf reforms

Major changes to the system of civil justice in England and Wales took effect in 1999, bringing in new **procedure rules** for the High Court and County Courts. The reform of civil justice was first proposed by Lord Woolf in his 1996 report *Access to Justice*.

Under the reforms, the Courts have the power to control every aspect of the litigation process, shifting responsibility away from the litigants and their advisers. This affects a wide range of commercial disputes.

The new procedures are designed to lead to **quicker and less confrontational** settlement of disputes preferably at the beginning of a case, to encourage parties to consider **alternative methods** of dispute resolution, and to avoid the excessive expense of litigation, which Lord Bingham has called 'a cancer eating at the heart of the administration of justice'.

(a)   The court allocates cases to 'tracks' – the **small claims track**, the **fast track** or the **multi-track**.

(b)   The small claims track deals with claims of not more than £5,000.

(c)   The fast track limit is £15,000. This is a strictly limited procedure, designed to take cases to trial within a short but reasonable timescale. Trials should take only half a day. The fast track is likely to include personal injury, building, consumer and neighbour dispute cases.

(d)   Larger claims are allocated to the multi-track. This spans both High Court and county court cases, and covers most commercial claims. There is an initial 'case management conference' to encourage parties to settle the dispute or to consider alternative dispute resolution (such as mediation or arbitration).

(e)   The trial judge in a multi-track trial sets a budget and a final timetable for the trial.

The court's management of a case is achieved by the setting up of **codes of practice** with which the parties must comply, and which will ensure effective exchange of information **before the proceedings begin**.

Litigants will have to be much better prepared before going to court. One consequence of this is that costs of litigation will be largely known in advance. For example, the court's permission will now be needed to call expert witnesses, and the court can compel the parties to use a single joint witness. The names of court documents and applications are being changed to make them more user friendly. A new procedure will allow for quick disposal of inadequate cases.

There will be a new senior judge with overall responsibility for civil justice, to be known as the **Head of Civil Justice**. His appointment is designed to raise the status of civil justice, which has long been in the shadow of the criminal justice system.

3.3   The High Court

The **High Court** is organised into three divisions.

- Queen's Bench
- Chancery Division
- Family Division

Queen's Bench Division

(a) *Civil jurisdiction*

The Queen's Bench Division (QBD) deals mainly with common law matters such as actions based on contract or tort It is therefore the most relevant court to this unit. It also has a supervisory role over other courts. It is the largest of the three divisions, having 54 judges. It includes a separate **Admiralty Court** to deal with shipping matters, and a **Commercial Court** which specialises in commercial cases.

(b) *Supervisory role*

The QBD can issue orders to other lower courts to take or desist from particular actions.

(c) *Criminal (appellate) jurisdiction*

The division hears some appeals from the magistrates' courts and the Crown Courts.

Chancery Division

This division deals with traditional equity matters.

- Trusts and mortgages
- Revenue matters
- Bankruptcy (though outside London this is a county court subject)
- Disputed wills and administration of estates of deceased persons
- Partnership and company matters

There is a separate **Companies Court** within the division which deals with liquidations and other company proceedings.

Family Division

This division deals with matrimonial cases, family property cases, and proceedings relating to children (wardship, guardianship, adoption, legitimacy etc). The division hears appeals from magistrates' courts and the county court on family matters.

Appeals

Appeals are made from the High Court as follows.

(a) *Civil cases*

Appeals may be made to the **Court of Appeal (Civil Division)** or to the **House of Lords,** under what is known as the (rarely used) **'leapfrog'** procedure. For the leapfrog procedure to be followed, all parties must give their consent to it, and the case must involve a point of law of general public importance.

(b) *Criminal cases*

Appeals are made direct to the House of Lords where the case has reached the High Court on appeal from a magistrates' court or from the Crown Court.

Staffing

The High Court is staffed by no more than 98 puisne (pronounced 'puny') judges, who must be barristers of at least ten years' standing. QBD is presided over by the Lord Chief Justice. Chancery has 13 judges and is presided over by the Lord Chancellor. Family Division has 16 judges and its President presides.

3.4 Criminal structure

The diagram below sets out the **English criminal court structure.**

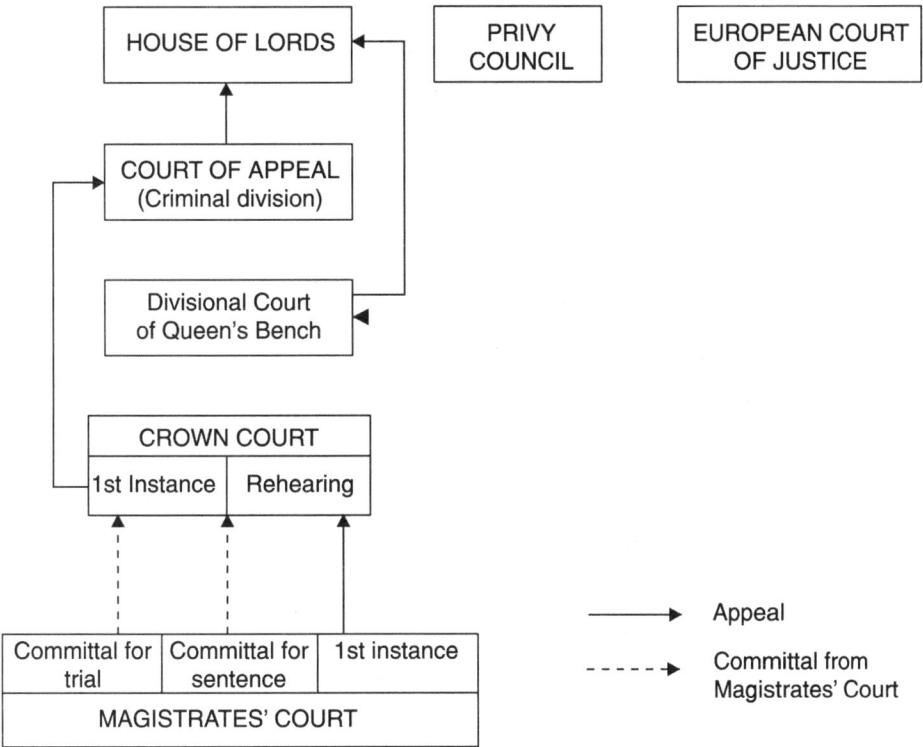

3.5 Magistrates' courts

Magistrates' courts are the inferior criminal courts. In addition they exercise certain family law, administrative law and minor civil functions.

Criminal jurisdiction

Magistrates' courts deal with **criminal cases** as follows.

(a) They try summarily (without a jury) all minor offences.

(b) They conduct **committal proceedings,** which are preliminary investigations of the prosecution case, when the offence is triable only on **indictment** (by a Crown Court). For example, all cases of murder, although it is a serious offence, will start in the magistrates' court and then be committed to the Crown Court.

Definitions

Summary offences are minor crimes, only triable summarily in magistrates' courts, for example speeding, pickpocketing.

Indictable offences are more serious offences that can only be heard in a Crown Court. Examples include murder and arson. Some offences are '**triable either way**'. This means that the defendant can choose whether to be tried summarily by the magistrates, or by a jury in the Crown Court. Some types of burglary or robbery are triable either way.

The maximum penalties which **magistrates** may impose on a defendant convicted summarily of a criminal offence are **six months' imprisonment** or a **fine (or compensation to victim) of up to £5,000**. However, they can commit a person convicted of a summary offence to Crown Court for sentencing, so that a larger penalty may be imposed.

Civil jurisdiction

Magistrates' civil jurisdiction includes family proceedings (financial provision for parties to a marriage and children, the custody or supervision of children and guardianship, and adoption orders), various types of licensing, and enforcement of local authority charges and rates, for example the early opening of pubs in the UK during the Rugby World Cup in 2003.

Appeals

A defendant convicted on a **criminal charge** in a magistrates' court has a general right to a rehearing by a Crown Court.

On **family matters**, appeals are to a divisional court of the Family Division of the High Court.

Staffing

Lay magistrates are not legally qualified and they sit part-time. They are appointed by the Lord Chancellor and are assisted by a legally qualified clerk, who must be a solicitor or barrister of at least five years' standing. **Stipendiary magistrates** must be solicitors or barristers of at least seven years' standing. They are full time magistrates and sit in cities. Lay magistrates sit two or three to a court, while stipendiary magistrates sit alone.

Activity 4 (10 mins)

Agatha is being prosecuted for an offence that is triable either way. She elects to be tried summarily in the magistrates' court, as she thinks that this will ensure that she cannot be sentenced to more than six months imprisonment or fined more than £5,000. Is she right?

Give reasons for your answer.

3.6 The Crown Court

The Crown Court is theoretically a single court forming part of the **Supreme Court,** but in fact it comprises **local courts** in large towns and also the **Central Criminal Court** (the Old Bailey, scene of many high profile trials) in London.

Criminal jurisdiction

It tries all indictable offences with a jury and hears appeals and deals with committals for sentencing from magistrates' courts.

Civil jurisdiction

The Crown Court deals with a few types of civil cases, being appeals from the magistrates' court on matters of betting, gaming and licensing.

Appeals

From the Crown Court there is a right of appeal on criminal matters to the Criminal Division of the Court of Appeal. An appeal on a point of law may also be made to a Divisional Court of the Queen's Bench Division.

Staffing

A High Court Judge, a circuit judge or a recorder may sit in the Crown Court, depending on the nature of the offence being tried. Sometimes lay magistrates also sit. All indictable offences will be heard by a judge with a jury of between 10 and 12 persons.

3.7 The Court of Appeal

The two branches of the law, civil and criminal, come together in the Court of Appeal and the High Court.

Civil Division

The Civil Division of the Court of Appeal can hear appeals from the High Court, county courts, and from certain other courts and special tribunals. It reviews the record of the evidence in the lower court and the legal arguments put before it. It may uphold or reverse the earlier decision or order a new trial.

Criminal Division

The Criminal Division of the Court of Appeal hears appeals from the Crown Court. It may also be invited to review a criminal case by the Home Secretary or to consider a point of law at the request of the Attorney General. Such appeals can have a widespread effect: in early 2004 a decision of the Court of Appeal meant that the government undertook to review over 250 cases of suspected child murder, which could in fact have been cot death.

Appeals

Appeals lie to the House of Lords, with the leave of the House of Lords or the Court of Appeal, on a point of law.

Staffing

There are 29 **Lord Justices of Appeal,** promoted from the High Court. Three judges normally sit together. In the Criminal Division, the **Lord Chief Justice** presides. In the Civil Division the **Master of the Rolls** presides.

3.8 The House of Lords

The House of Lords has two separate roles, and it is important that these are not confused.

(a) It has a **legislative role,** as one of the two Houses of Parliament. It approves, delays or argues against, all proposed Acts of Parliament.

(b) It has a **judicial role,** as the highest appeal court of the legal system, hearing appeals from both the civil and criminal divisions of the Court of Appeal.

Judges are usually promoted from the Court of Appeal to be members of the House of Lords. They are known as **Lords of Appeal in Ordinary,** or **Law Lords.** Five judges normally sit together, though there may only be three.

3.9 European courts

As we shall see in the next chapter, European Community law has a significant impact on English law. The ultimate courts of appeal in the UK system are the European courts.

European Court of Human Rights

Since the Human Rights Act 1998 came into operation in 2000, the European Court of Human Rights is the ultimate appeal court on cases on human rights, which must first be heard in the UK system.

European Court of Justice

This is the major European court and it is the final court of appeal in the UK for all other cases.

Activity 5 (10 mins)

List the court (or courts) to which an appeal may be made from each of the following:

(a) The county court
(b) The High Court (civil cases)

(Refer to the court structure diagrams in sections 3.1 and 3.4)

4 OTHER MEANS OF RESOLVING DISPUTES

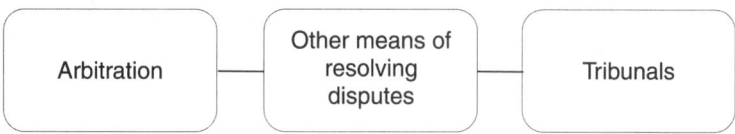

4.1 Tribunals

Employment tribunals

Employment tribunals (formerly industrial tribunals) have a wide jurisdiction over most disputes between **employee and employer**. Each tribunal is staffed by a legally qualified **chairman** and two other persons, one representing the employer and one representing the employee. Here are some examples of typical cases.

- Disputes about redundancy pay
- Complaints of unfair dismissal
- Questions as to terms of contracts of employment
- Equal pay claims
- Appeals against health and safety notices
- Complaints about sex and race discrimination

There is a right of appeal to the **Employment Appeal Tribunal**.

Employment Appeal Tribunal

This is a court of equal status with the High Court. It was established by the Employment Protection Act 1975. It hears appeals from tribunals mainly on employment matters.

A **High Court judge** and two **lay assessors** from a panel appointed on the Lord Chancellor's recommendation sit. From the EAT there is a right of appeal to the Court of Appeal.

Social security appeal tribunals

A variety of cash benefits are available under the Social Security Act 1975 (including unemployment benefit, invalidity and sickness benefit and retirement pensions) and the Social Security Act 1986 (including income support, family credit and housing benefit). Questions may arise in the administration of these benefits. The Social Security appeal tribunals hear appeals arising from the adjudication process.

Lands Tribunal

This tribunal deals with disputes over the value of property, for example for compulsory purchase. It is usually composed of three members, being experienced lawyers and qualified valuation experts.

Supervision of tribunals

The working of the system of tribunals is supervised by a **Council on Tribunals**. In many instances there is a statutory right to appeal from a tribunal to a higher court on points of law. The High Court may also make prerogative orders to prevent or remedy errors and injustices.

4.2 Arbitration

This is increasingly becoming a popular alternative to litigation in the courts, and it is now quite common for contracts, especially large commercial contracts, to contain provision for voluntary arbitration in the event of a dispute arising between the parties to the contract. This can be very helpful as referring the dispute to arbitration means that it will be handled by an independent expert who fully understands the legal ramifications. It also provides advantages such as privacy for the parties involved.

Proceedings in arbitration are less adversarial and confrontational in nature than court hearings (where one party is 'opposed' to the other) so it is more likely that a compromise will be found, meaning that the concept of 'winners and losers' is less pronounced.

Unless otherwise agreed, a hearing before an arbitrator follows the same essential procedure as in a court of law. However, following the Arbitration Act 1996, the arbitrators and parties can settle on the **form** of the arbitration.

The Arbitration Act 1996

The Arbitration Act 1996 aimed to introduce **greater speed and flexibility** into the arbitration process, in particular by conferring upon the parties the right to make their own agreement on virtually all aspects of the arbitration (s 1). It contains provisions for the **appointment and removal** of arbitrators, and the power to appoint **experts** (s 37), advisers and assessors. It turned the courts' role into a **supervisory** rather than an interventionist one. Under this Act, the parties may choose to dispense with formal hearings and strict rules of evidence and procedure (s 46).

Under the 1996 Act, an arbitration agreement is a **separate agreement** which can outlive the original contract that gave rise to the arbitration proceedings.

The main advantage of the arbitration procedure is **privacy**, since the public and the press have no right to attend a hearing before an arbitrator.

Compulsory arbitration

In addition to voluntary arbitration as described above, compulsory arbitration may be enforced in the following circumstances.

(a) Certain statutes (Acts of Parliament) provide for arbitration on disputes arising out of the provision of the statute.

(b) The High Court may order that a case of a technical nature shall be tried (or investigated with report back to the court) by an Official Referee or other arbitrator.

(c) A county court may order that a small claim (not exceeding £5,000) shall be referred to arbitration, under the small claims court procedure.

Chapter roundup

- Law is a fundamental part of a civilised society and governs the relationships between individuals among themselves and between individuals and the state.

- People are prosecuted under the criminal law for offences committed against the state, and a penalty is imposed.

- Individuals (or companies) sue each other under the civil law to receive compensation for some kind of loss or damage suffered. The purpose is not punishment but the righting of a wrong.

- There is a hierarchy of civil and criminal courts. In broad terms those lower down in the hierarchy have a right to appeal to those above. The operation of the civil courts depends largely on the financial value of the case under consideration.

- Going to court is not the only means of resolving a dispute. Tribunals deal with specific cases involving employment and other specialised areas, and arbitration provides a highly effective alternative to litigation.

Quick quiz

1   Give two examples each of public and private law.

2   What degree of proof is required in a civil case?

3   In which court will a criminal case start to go through the legal process?

4   What matters are dealt with by the Small Claims Court?

5   Which court hears appeals arising from decisions of the Court of Appeal?

8   What are the advantages of arbitration over court action?

Answers to quick quiz

1   Public law: criminal law
                     constitutional law
    Private law: contract law
                     law of tort

2   Proof on the balance of probability.

3   Magistrate's court.

4   Small contract and other claims worth less than £5,000.

5   The House of Lords.

6   Reference to detail
    Use of experts
    Privacy
    Compromise

NOTES

Answers to activities

1. Nothing can be proved beyond **all** doubt

2. Martin could be prosecuted under the criminal law for speeding, and also sued by Andrew under the civil law for damages for the damage caused to Andrew's house.

3. The case for £10,000 would probably be heard in the County Court. If the amount involved was £3,000 it would probably be dealt with under the small claims procedure.

4. This will not ensure a lower sentence, as Agatha could be convicted in the magistrates' court but then committed to the Crown Court for sentencing.

5. (a) The Court of Appeal (Civil Division) or the High Court
    (b) The Court of Appeal (Civil Division) or the House of Lords

---

Assignment

Since the content of this chapter is introductory background reading, and you will not be tested in detail on the contents in any assignment, we do not include a specific assignment for this chapter.

However, remember that you will encounter many of the terms and concepts introduced here in your later studies, and you may be expected to apply them in assignments at that stage.

Now that you have started to study law, look out for reports of legal cases (both criminal and civil) in the newspapers. Look for practical applications of the law that you have been learning.

Chapter 2 :
SOURCES OF LAW

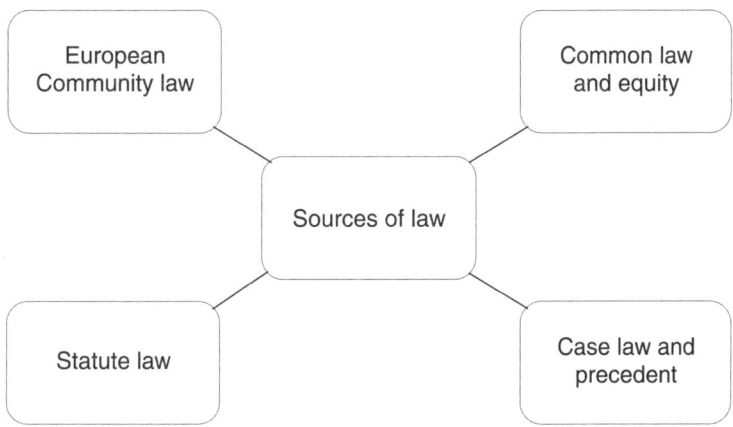

Introduction

There are three main sources of law with which you need to be familiar if you are fully to understand the detailed areas of the law which are covered in the forthcoming chapters. The first is case law, which is the law that is created as a result of the decisions of the courts. The second is statute, which is the law created by Acts of Parliament. The third is EC law. It is important for you to understand the role of EC law in the UK.

Throughout this course book, you will find references to cases to illustrate the legal principles and rules which you will learn, and also to statute (shown for example as *Companies Act 1985 S368*). You will find reference to EC regulations, which have the force of law in the UK, and directives which must be implemented by national legislation.

Case law and statute are often referred to as the **legal** sources of law. There are also two important **historical** sources of law, common law and equity, from which much of case law springs, and we shall consider these first.

Your objectives

In this chapter you will learn about the following.

    (a)   The development of the common law

    (b)   The development of equity

    (c)   The doctrine of judicial precedent and when it is not applied

    (d)   The importance of legislation

    (e)   How legislation is made

    (f)   The importance of delegated legislation

    (g)   The role of EC law

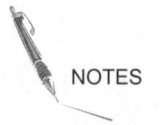

As with the previous chapter, you should regard this as background reading. You will not be tested on this in your assignments, but a familiarity with it will help you to understand the law and terminology you will study in subsequent chapters. Additionally the contents of this chapter are directly relevant to Unit 25 English Legal System, should you choose to pursue the Law endorsed title route.

1   COMMON LAW AND EQUITY

English law has developed in an unbroken progression over a period of some 900 years. English law's historical sources are those procedures, rules and ways of thinking which have given rise to today's current sources of law. A legal problem may be decided on the rules of the legal sources, but these in turn (particularly judicial precedent) have been derived from the historical sources of **common law** and **equity**.

1.1   Common law

Definition

> **Common Law**: the body of legal rules developed by the common law courts and now embodied in legal decisions.

At the time of the Norman Conquest in 1066 there was no system of law common to the whole country. Rules of local custom were applied by local manorial courts. To improve the system, the King sent royal commissioners on tour (circuit) to different parts of the realm to deal with crimes and civil disputes. In time the commissioners developed rules of law, selected from the differing local customs which they had encountered, as a common law which they applied uniformly in all trials (before the King's courts) throughout the kingdom.

Definitions

> **Claimant**: the person who complains or brings an action asking the court for relief (used to be called the plaintiff).
>
> **Defendant**: the person against whom a civil action is brought or who is prosecuted for a criminal offence.

The procedure of common law could be unsatisfactory. A claimant might lose his case owing to a minor technicality of wording, be frustrated by specious defences, deliberate delay or corruption, or find himself unable to enforce a judgement given in his favour because there was no suitable common law remedy.

1.2 Equity

Definition

> **Equity**: a source of English law consisting of those rules which emerged from the Court of Chancery.

Citizens who could not obtain redress for grievances in the common law courts petitioned the King to obtain relief by direct royal intervention.

The principles on which the Chancellor (on behalf of the King) decided points were based on fair dealing between two individuals as equals. These principles became known as **equity**. The system of equity, developed and administered by the Court of Chancery, was not an alternative to the common law, but a method of **adding to and improving on the common law**. This interaction of common law and equity produced three major changes.

(a) **New rights**. Equity recognised and protected rights for which the common law gave no safeguards. If, for example, Sam transferred property to the legal ownership of Tom to pay the income of the property to Ben (in modern law Tom is a trustee for Ben), the common law simply recognised that Tom was the owner of the property and ignored Tom's obligations to Ben. Equity recognised that Tom was the owner of the property at common law but insisted, as a matter of justice and good conscience, that Tom must comply with the terms of the trust imposed by Sam (the settlor) and pay the income to Ben (the beneficiary).

(b) **Better procedure**. Equity could be more effective than common law in bringing a disputed matter to a decision.

(c) **Better remedies**. The standard common law remedy for the successful claimant was the award of monetary compensation, damages, for his loss. Equity was able to order the defendant to do what he had agreed to do (specific performance), to abstain from wrongdoing (injunction), to alter a document so that it reflected the parties' true intentions (rectification) or to restore the pre-contract position (rescission).

Definition

> **Specific performance**: an equitable remedy in which the court orders the defendant to perform his side of a contract.
>
> **Injunction**: an equitable remedy in which the court orders the other party to a contract to observe negative restrictions, for example not to go to another person's house.
>
> **Rectification**: an equitable remedy in which the court can order a document to be altered so that it reflects the parties' true intentions.
>
> **Rescission**: an equitable remedy through which a contract is cancelled or rejected and the parties are restored to their pre-contract condition, as if it had never been entered into.

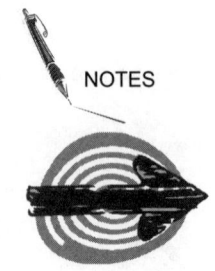

You will see all of these equitable remedies in action (as well as the common law remedy of damages) when you study both contract and tort.

Equitable maxims

The development of equity was based on a number of equitable maxims (or principles).

These are still applied today if an equitable remedy is sought. The following are examples.

(a) **He who comes to equity must come with clean hands.** To be fairly treated, the claimant must have acted fairly himself. For example, in the case *D and C Builders v Rees 1966* the defendant could not plead a special defence called equitable estoppel because she had tried to take advantage of the claimant's financial difficulties.

(b) **Equality is equity**. The law attempts to play fair and redress the balance; hence what is available to one person must be available to another. As an example, equity does not allow the remedy of specific performance to be granted against a minor (ie a person under the age of 18), and it does not allow a minor to benefit from the remedy either.

(c) **Equity looks at the intent, not the form**. However a person may try to pretend that he is doing something in the correct form, equity will look at what he is actually trying to achieve. For example, if an agreed damages clause in a contract is not a genuine estimate of likely loss, equity will treat the clause as a penalty clause, and it is less likely to be awarded to the injured party.

The relationship between common law and equity

Until the 1870s, common law and equity as sources of law had to be administered in separate courts. However, the Judicature Acts of the 1870s enabled them to be administered in the same court, and a judge is able to apply whichever principles he thinks fit.

In the case of a conflict between the two, however, equity will prevail. It is sometimes described as 'a gloss on the common law' in that where a common law decision would produce an unfair, or inequitable, result, equity can be applied to avoid that outcome.

2 CASE LAW AND PRECEDENT

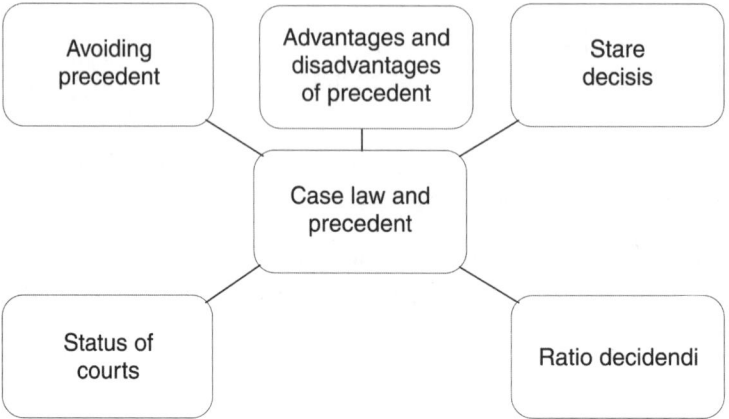

As noted above, the development of common law and equity has led to one of the main legal sources of law, case law, and has an influence on much of the other main source, legislation.

2.1 Stare decisis

Both common law and equity are the product of decisions in the courts. They are judge-made law but based on a principle of consistency. Once a matter of principle has been decided (by one of the higher courts) it becomes a precedent. In any later case to which that principle is relevant the same principle should (subject to certain exceptions) be applied. This doctrine of consistency, following precedent, is expressed in the maxim **stare decisis**, 'to stand by a decision'.

Judges inevitably create law. Sometimes an Act of Parliament will deliberately vest a wide discretion in the judiciary. In other cases there may be no statutory provision and no existing precedent relevant to the particular dispute. Even so, the doctrine of judicial precedent is based on the view that it is not the function of a judge to make law, but to **decide** cases in accordance with existing rules, ie to apply the law.

It is generally accepted that consistency is an important feature of a good decision-making process. Similar cases should be treated in the same way. However, the passage of time, or changing circumstances, may cause a case to offer a solution which no longer appears just. One of the main functions of the higher courts is to give an authoritative decision on disputed questions of law. A court's decision is expected to be consistent (or at least not unjustifiably inconsistent) with previous decisions and to provide an opinion which the parties, and others, can use to direct their future relationships. This is the basis of the system of **judicial precedent**.

Judicial precedent depends on the following.

    (a)   There must be adequate and reliable reports of earlier decisions.

    (b)   There must be rules for extracting from an earlier decision on one set of facts the legal principle to be applied in reaching a decision on a different set of facts.

        (i)   The principle must be a proposition of law.

        (ii)   It must form part of the ratio decidendi of the case.

        (iii)   The material facts of each case must be the same.

    (c)   Precedents must be classified into those which are binding and those which are merely persuasive. This depends primarily on the respective status of the preceding court and the later one.

2.2 Ratio decidendi

Definitions

> **Ratio decidendi**: the reason for a decision.
>
> **Obiter dicta**: statements made by a judge 'by the way'.

A judgement will start with a description of the facts of the case and probably a review of earlier precedents and possible alternative theories. The judge will then make statements of law applicable to the legal problems raised by the material facts. Provided these statements are the basis for the decision, they are known as the **ratio decidendi** of the case. The ratio decidendi (reason for deciding) is the vital element which **binds future judges**.

If a judge's statements of legal principle do not form the basis of the decision, or if his statements are not based on the existing material facts but on hypothetical facts, they are known as **obiter dicta** (said by the way). A later court may respect such statements, but it is not bound to follow them. They are only of **persuasive authority**.

It is not always easy to identify the ratio decidendi. The same judgement may appear to contain contradictory views of the law in different passages. In decisions of appeal courts, where there are three or even five separate judgements, the members of the court may reach the same conclusion but give different reasons. The ratio may also be mingled with obiter statements. Many judges help by indicating in their speeches which comments are ratio and which are obiter.

Activity 1   **(10 mins)**

A case hinges upon whether clementines are oranges. The judgement contains the remark 'clementines are oranges, just as peanuts are nuts'. How does this remark illustrate the distinction between ratio decidendi and obiter dicta?

Distinguishing the facts

Although there may arguably be a finite number of legal principles to consider when deciding a case, there are necessarily an infinite variety of facts which may be presented. Apart from identifying the ratio decidendi of an earlier case, it is also necessary to consider how far the facts of the previous and the latest case are similar. Facts are never identical. If the differences appear significant the court may 'distinguish' the earlier case on the facts and thereby avoid following it as a precedent.

2.3 The status of courts

Look back at the diagrams of the court structures in Paragraphs 3.1 and 3.4 of the last chapter. Generally the higher the court the more binding its decisions. A court's status has a significant effect on whether its decisions are binding, persuasive or disregarded.

(a)   The House of Lords stands at the apex of the domestic judicial system. Its decisions are binding on all other English courts. The House of Lords generally regards itself as bound by its own earlier decisions but it reserves the right to depart from its own precedents in exceptional cases.

(b)   The Court of Appeal's decisions are binding on all English courts except the House of Lords. It is bound by its own previous decisions and by those of the House of Lords.

(c)   A single High Court judge is bound by decisions of higher courts but not by a decision of another High Court judge sitting alone (though he would treat it as strong persuasive authority). When two or more High Court judges sit

together as a Divisional Court, their decisions are binding on any other Divisional Court (and on a single High Court judge sitting alone).

(d) Lower courts (the Crown Court, county courts and magistrates' courts) do not make precedents, and their decisions are not usually reported. They are bound by decisions of the higher courts.

(e) If, in a case before the House of Lords there is a dispute about a point of European Community (EC) law, it must be referred to the European Court of Justice for a ruling. English courts are also required to take account of principles laid down by the Court of Justice in so far as these are relevant. The Court of Justice does not, however, create or follow precedents as such.

Apart from binding precedents as described above, reported decisions of any court (even if lower in status) may be treated as persuasive precedents: they may be (but need not be) followed in a later case.

Overruling a precedent

A court of higher status is not only free to disregard the decision of a court of lower status in an earlier case. It may also deprive it of authority and expressly overrule it. This does not affect the outcome as regards the defendant and claimant in the earlier decision; it only affects the precedents to be applied in later cases.

2.4 Avoiding precedent

Even if a precedent appears to be binding, a court may decline to follow it:

(a) By distinguishing the facts , that is, saying that this case is different.

(b) By declaring the ratio decidendi obscure, particularly when a decision by three or five judges gives as many different ratios

(c) By declaring that the previous decision was made *per incuriam*, that is, without taking account of some essential point of law, such as an important precedent

(d) By declaring the precedent to be in conflict with a fundamental principle of law

(e) By declaring the precedent to be too wide

(f) Because the earlier decision has been subsequently overruled by another court or by statute

Activity 2 **(10 mins)**

A brings an action against B and the case is finally settled in favour of B in the Court of Appeal. Fifteen years later C brings an action against D on similar but slightly different facts and the case of A v B is the only relevant precedent. If C v D reaches the House of Lords, consider whether the case of A v B is binding.

2.5 The advantages and disadvantages of precedent

Many of the strengths of judicial precedent also indicate some of its weaknesses. Generally the arguments revolve around the principles of consistency, clarity, flexibility and detail.

Consistency. The whole point of following binding precedent is that the law is decided fairly and predictably. In theory therefore it should be possible to avoid litigation because the result is a foregone conclusion. However, judges are often forced to make illogical distinctions to avoid an unfair result which, combined with the wealth of reported cases, serves to complicate the law.

Clarity. Following only the reasoning in ratio statements should lead to statements of principle for general application. In practice, however, the same judgement may be found to contain propositions which appear inconsistent with each other or with the precedent which the court purports to follow.

Flexibility. The real strength of the system lies in its ability to change with changing circumstances since it arises directly out of the actions of society. The counter argument is that the doctrine limits judges' discretion and they may be unable to avoid deciding in line with a precedent which produces an unfair result. Often the deficiency may only be remedied by passing a statute to correct the law's failings.

Detail. Precedents state how the law applies to facts, and it should be flexible enough to allow for details to be different, so that the law is all-encompassing. However, judges often distinguish cases on facts to avoid following a precedent. The wealth of detail is also a drawback in that it produces a vast body of reports which must be taken into account; again, though, statute can help by codifying rules developed in case law.

3 STATUTE LAW

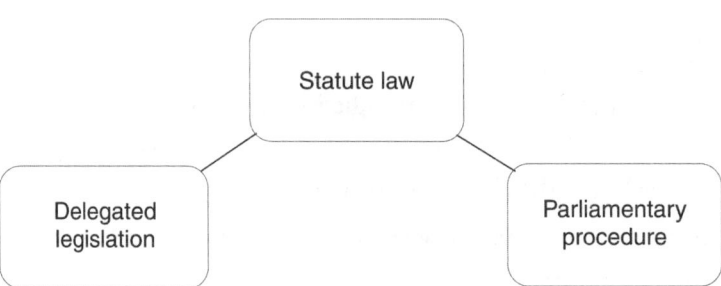

Legislation is enacted by Parliament. Until the UK entered the European Community (the EC) in 1973 the UK Parliament was completely sovereign: its law-making powers were unfettered.

Parliamentary sovereignty means that:

(a) Parliament is able to make the law as it sees fit. It may repeal earlier statutes, overrule case law developed in the courts or make new law on subjects which have not been regulated by law before.

(b) No Parliament can legislate so as to prevent a future Parliament changing the law.

(c) Judges are bound to apply the relevant statute law however distasteful to them it may be.

In practice, Parliament usually follows certain conventions which limit its freedom. It does not usually enact statutes which alter the law with retrospective effect or deprive citizens of their property without compensation.

3.1 Parliamentary procedure

A proposal for legislation is originally aired in public in a Government green paper. After comments are received a white paper is produced, which sets out the aim of the legislation. It is then put forward in draft form as a bill, and may be introduced into either the House of Commons or the House of Lords, the two Houses of Parliament. When the bill has passed through one House it must then go through the same stages in the other House.

In each House the successive stages of dealing with the bill are as follows.

(a) **First reading**: publication and introduction into the agenda: no debate.

(b) **Second reading**: debate on the general merits of the bill but no amendments at this stage.

(c) **Committee stage**: the bill is examined by a standing committee of about 20 members, representing the main parties and including some members at least who specialise in the relevant subject. The bill is examined section by section and may be amended. If the bill is very important all or part of the committee stage may be taken by the House as a whole sitting as a committee.

(d) **Report stage**: the bill as amended in committee is reported to the full House for approval. If the Government has undertaken in committee to reconsider various points it often puts forward its final amendments at this stage.

(e) **Third reading**: this is the final approval stage at which only verbal amendments may be made.

When it has passed through both Houses it is submitted for the **Royal Assent** which in practice is given on the Queen's behalf by a committee of the Lord Chancellor and two other peers. It then becomes an act of Parliament (or statute). It comes into effect at the start of the day on which Royal Assent is given, or (if the act itself so provides) at some other time or on a commencement date set by statutory instrument.

Most bills are public bills of general application, whether introduced by the Government or by a private member. They are referred to as **Government bills** or **private members' bills** respectively. Private members' bills are often brought on matters of conscience such as fox hunting.

If the House of Commons and the House of Lords disagree over the same bill, the House of Lords may delay the passing of the bill for a maximum of one year (except for financial measures, such as the annual Finance Act). In practice this can mean that some bills then fail for lack of time, such as recent attempts to ban hunting with dogs in England and Wales. The House of Lords may veto any bill which tries to extend the life of Parliament beyond five years.

NOTES

Activity 3	(10 mins)

Many countries have a bill of rights, which cannot be changed by normal legislative procedures. What aspect of Parliamentary sovereignty would make it difficult to give a bill of rights for the UK such a secure position?

3.2 Delegated legislation

Definition

Delegated legislation: rules of law made by subordinate bodies to whom the power to do so has been given by statute.

To save time in Parliament it is usual to set out the main principles in the body of an act as numbered sections and to relegate the details to schedules (at the end of the act) which need not be debated, though they are visible and take effect as part of the act. But even with this device there is a great deal which cannot conveniently be included in acts. It may, for example, be necessary, after an act has been passed, for the Government to consult interested parties and then produce regulations, having the force of the law, to implement the act, to fix commencement dates to bring the act into operation or to prescribe printed forms for use in connection with it. To provide for these and other matters a modern act usually contains a section by which power is given to a minister, or a public body such as a local authority, to make subordinate or delegated legislation for specified purposes only.

Delegated legislation appears in various forms. Ministerial powers are exercised by **statutory instrument** (including emergency powers of the Crown exercised by **Orders in Council**). Local authorities are given statutory powers to make **bye-laws**, which apply within a specific locality.

4 EUROPEAN COMMUNITY LAW

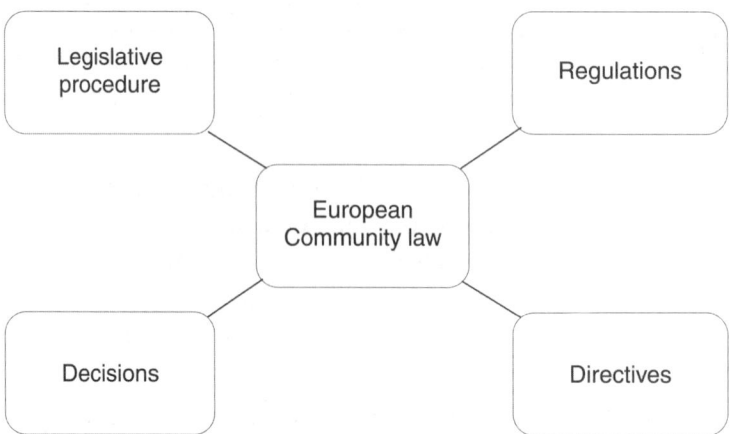

The European Community has recently increased to comprise 25 states by the admission of 10 additional nations, many from the former Eastern bloc.

PROFESSIONAL EDUCATION

The sources of Community Law may be described as primary or secondary. The **primary sources of law** are the foundation treaties themselves, such as the **First Treaty of Rome 1957**, which established the **EEC**

Secondary legislation takes three forms, with the Council and Commission being empowered to do the following:

- Make regulations
- Issue directives
- Take decisions

They may also make recommendations and deliver opinions although these are only persuasive in authority.

Direct applicability and direct effect

To understand the importance of regulations, directives and decisions, it is necessary to appreciate the distinction between **direct applicability** and **direct effect**.

Community law which is directly applicable in member states comes into force without any act of implementation by member states. Law has direct effect if it confers rights and imposes obligations directly on individuals.

4.1 Regulations

Regulations may be issued. They have the force of law in every EU state without need of national legislation. In this sense regulations are described as **directly applicable**. Their objective is to obtain uniformity of law throughout the EU.

Definition

> **Regulations** apply throughout the Community and they become part of the law of each member nation as soon as they come into force without the need for each country to make its own legislation.

Direct law-making of this type is generally restricted to matters within the basic aims of Treaty of Rome, such as the establishment of a single unrestricted market in the EC territory in manufactured goods. Many regulations are concerned with food and drink manufacture.

Acts of implementation are actually prohibited, in case a member state alters the scope of the regulation in question.

4.2 Directives

Definition

> **Directives** are issued to the governments of the EU member states requiring them within a specified period (usually two years) to alter the national laws of the state so that they conform to the directive.

BPP
PROFESSIONAL EDUCATION

Unit 5: Common Law I

Thus the Financial Services Act 1986 embodied certain directives on company securities and the Companies Act 1989 gives force to the Eighth Directive.

Until a directive is given effect by a UK statute it does not usually affect legal rights and obligations of individuals. The wording of a directive may be cited in legal proceedings, but generally **statutory interpretation has been a matter for the UK courts**. However, as noted above, under the Human Rights Act 1998, the courts are now required to interpret UK legislation in a way which is compatible with the European Convention on Human Rights.

4.3 Decisions

Decisions of an administrative nature are made by the European Commission in Brussels.

Definition

> A **decision** may be addressed to a state, person or a company and is immediately binding, but only on the recipient.

4.4 Legislative procedure

Proposals for EC legislation are drafted by the Commission. These drafts are referred to member states for comments. The directives are also debated in the preparatory stage by the European Parliament. The final stage is the consideration of a directive by the Council of Ministers. The Council authorises the issue of the directive and the member states must then alter their law accordingly.

Chapter roundup

- Case law is the application of reported cases to later cases.

- Decided cases can fix the law for the purposes of future cases heard before certain courts, through the doctrine of precedent.

- The binding element in an earlier decision is the ratio decidendi, not the obiter dicta.

- The House of Lords binds all courts except itself. The Court of Appeal and a Divisional Court of the High Court bind themselves and all lower courts.

- A court can avoid following a precedent on several grounds.

- Statute law is made by Parliament, which, subject to the UK's membership of the European Community, has unfettered legislative powers.

- Much detailed legislation is delegated to Government departments exercising powers conferred by Acts of Parliament.

- The European Commission is a significant source of UK law.

- EC law is primary (the foundation treaties) and secondary (regulations and directives).

- Regulations are directly applicable, that is, they have force of law in EC states, without the need for national legislation.

- Directives must generally be implemented by national laws. They are a significant method of importing EC law into the UK.

Quick quiz

1. How was the Common Law first developed?

2. Give some examples of equitable maxims.

3. Can obiter dicta in a case have any influence on the outcome of subsequent cases?

4. What does it mean to say that a court's decision was taken per incuriam?

5. What is meant by Parliamentary sovereignty?

6. Why is delegated legislation useful?

Answers to quick quiz

1. Through justices sent by the King to administer the same law to everyone.

2. 'He who comes to equity must come with clean hands'

   'Equality is equity'

   'Equity looks to the intent rather than the form' (para 1.2)

3. It can be persuasive, but it is not binding. (para 2.2)

4. Without taking some essential point into account. (para 2.4)

5   Parliament can make any law, but cannot prevent a future parliament from changing the law. Judges are bound by parliament.

6   To enable governments to introduce all legislation needed, otherwise there would not be enough time.

Answers to activities

1   'Clementines are oranges' is the ratio decidendi (ie the decision in the case). 'Peanuts are nuts' is an obiter dictum, an additional comment which is not central.

2   The House of Lords in C v D could disregard the Court of Appeal decision in A v B or even over-rule it. Alternatively the case A v B might be distinguished on its facts.

3   No Parliament can bind its successors.

Assignment

Since the content of this chapter is introductory background reading, and you will not be tested in detail on the contents in any assignment, we do not include a specific assignment for this chapter.

However, remember that you will encounter many of the terms and concepts introduced here in your later studies, and you may be expected to apply them in assignments at that stage.

As suggested at the end of chapter 1, keep an eye on the newspapers for legal news, especially, for example on aspects such as the expansion of the European Union and the issue of sovereignty.

PART A

ESSENTIAL ELEMENTS OF A VALID CONTRACT

Chapter 3 :

INTRODUCTION TO THE LAW OF CONTRACT

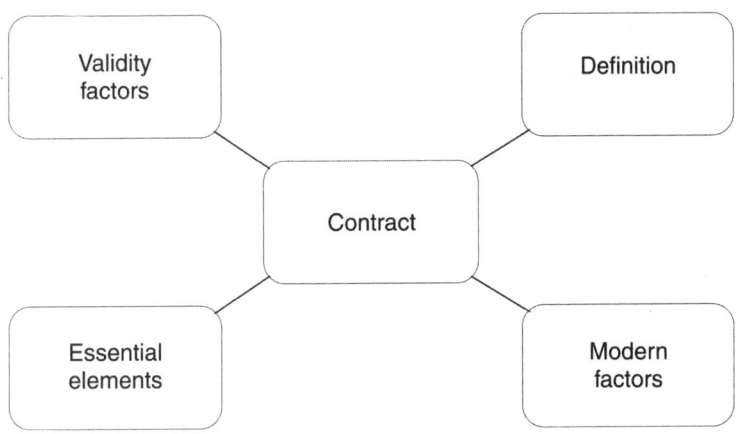

Introduction

A contract is an agreement which legally binds the parties to it. Consider the contracts that you may have entered into as an individual, when buying a house for example, or starting work. Similarly, a business will enter into contracts when it deals with property or takes on new staff.

Restrictions on the individual's freedom to make contracts have been developed to protect the disadvantaged, particularly in their dealings with large or monopolistic organisations. An example is the Sale of Goods Act 1979, which implies certain terms into contracts for the sale of goods, which cannot be excluded in consumer sales. A seller is bound by these terms even though he has never agreed to them, or may never have even thought of them.

Your objectives

In this chapter you will learn about the following.

    (a)   The nature of a contract

    (b)   The classification of contracts

    (c)   The essentials of a valid contract

From this point onwards, you are dealing with precise topics within the Edexcel guidelines, rather than background reading.

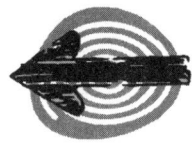

1 DEFINITION

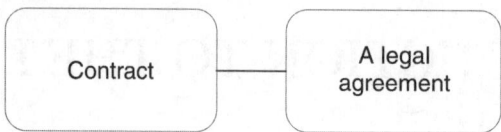

A contract may be defined as an **agreement which legally binds the parties**

A party to a contract is bound because he has **agreed** to be bound. The underlying theory, then, is that a contract is the outcome of 'consenting minds'. Parties are not judged by what is in their minds, but by what they have said, written or done.

2 MODERN FACTORS

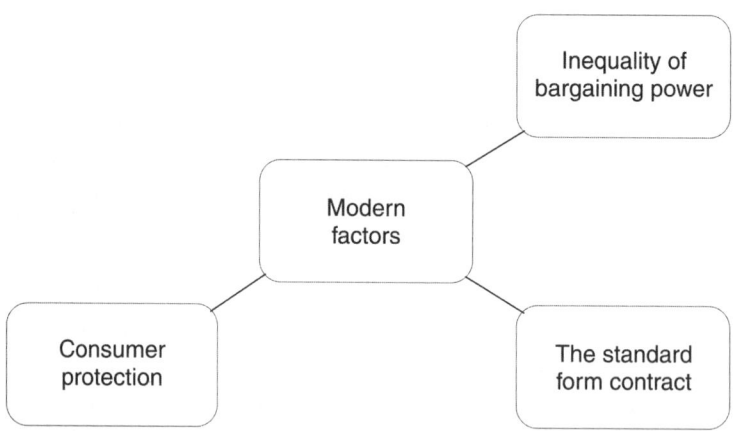

Many principles of modern contract law are strongly influenced by the events and important cases of the nineteenth century. However, a number of **developments in the twentieth century** should be brought into consideration.

2.1 Inequality of bargaining power

It is almost invariably the case that the two parties to a contract bring with them differing levels of bargaining power. The law will intervene only where the stronger party takes unfair advantage of his position.

2.2 The standard form contract

Mass production and nationalisation have led to the standard form contract.

Definition

> The **standard form** contract is a standard document prepared by many large organisations and setting out the terms on which they contract with their customers. The individual must usually take it or leave it: he does not really 'agree' to it. For example, a customer has to accept his supply of electricity on the electricity board's terms; individuals cannot negotiate discounts.

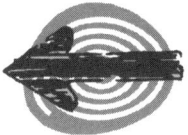

One of the main problems with standard form contracts occurs when the dominant party tries to exclude liability for the terms in the contract. The legislation protecting consumers in such situations, the Unfair Contract Terms Act, is covered in Chapter 7.

2.3 Consumer protection

In the second half of the twentieth century, there was a surge of interest in **consumer matters** mainly because of mass production and aggressive marketing. There is a greater need for **consumer protection**. Consumer interests are now served by consumer protection agencies, which include government departments (the **Office of Fair Trading**) and independent bodies (the **Consumers' Association**) and legislation.

Public policy sometimes requires that the freedom of contract should be modified. For example, the Consumer Credit Act 1974 and the Unfair Contract Terms Act 1977 both regulate the extent to which contracts can contain certain terms.

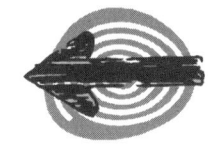

Consumer protection is covered in detail in Unit 26, Business Law.

3 ESSENTIAL ELEMENTS

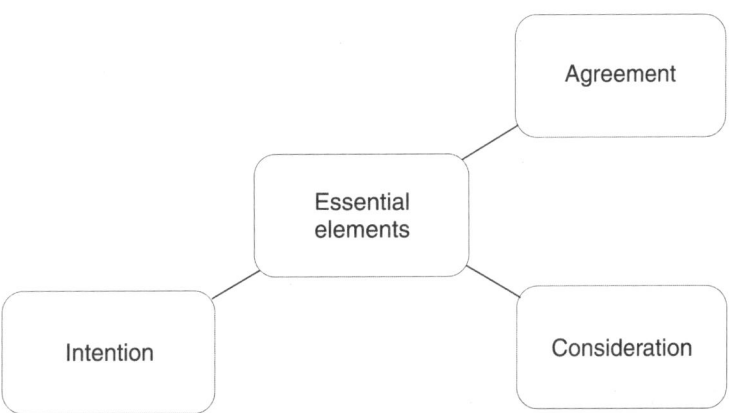

In order to be valid and enforceable by the law, a contract must contain certain key elements. These are as follows.

3.1 Agreement

The first essential feature of a contract is that the parties have made an agreement. This is determined by the rules of **offer** and **acceptance** which will be outlined in Chapter 4.

3.2 Consideration

The second essential element is that the agreement, or the obligations assumed by each party, must be supported by consideration from the other party. We will cover the rules of consideration in Chapter 5.

3.3 Intention to create legal relations

The last essential element is that the parties to the agreement intend that their promises be legally binding. In Chapter 6, we discuss intention to create legal relations and the capacity of certain groups of people to enter contracts.

4 VALIDITY FACTORS

If one of the three essential elements of contract is not present, there is no contract. However, even if all three essential elements are present, the validity of a contract may be affected. The validity of a contract may be affected by the following factors.

(a) **Form.** The general rule is that a contract may be in any form (written or oral, for example). However, a minority of contracts have to be made in a particular form.

(b) **Genuine consent.** The validity of a contract may be affected if a person has been misled into a contract, or if the parties have come to agreement, but are actually at cross-purposes, ie one of them is mistaken as to the precise nature of the contract.

(c) **Capacity.** some persons, for example children, only have limited capacity to enter into contracts.

(d) **Content.** A contract must be complete and precise in its terms. We will discuss this in Chapter 8.

(e) **Legality.** The courts will not enforce a contract which is deemed to be illegal or contrary to public policy.

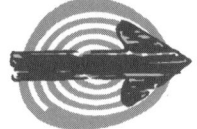

Genuine consent and legality do not fall within the parameters of the Guidelines for this Unit. Instead they are covered in detail in the endorsed title law route, in Unit 27, Common Law II.

4.1 Invalid contracts

A contract which is affected by such 'vitiating factors' exists, but may be **void, voidable** or **unenforceable**. It is important that you understand the difference between these terms.

Definitions

(a) A **void contract** is **not a contract** at all. The parties are not bound by it and if they transfer property under it they can sometimes (unless it is also an illegal contract) recover their goods even from a third party.

For example, A sells goods to B, who sells them on to C. B then fails to pay A for the goods and disappears without trace. If A can demonstrate that he was genuinely mistaken as to the identity of B and would not have dealt with him had he known who B really was, then A can recover the goods which were subject to the original contract from C. This is because the law takes the view in such a situation that the original contract between A and B was no contract at all and of no effect.

Therefore C, who was an innocent third party acting in good faith, has to return the goods to A and either bear the loss or find and sue B.

(b) A **voidable contract** is a **contract which one party may avoid**, that is terminate at his option. The contract is treated as valid unless and until it is avoided. Property transferred before avoidance is usually irrecoverable from a third party.

For example A sells goods to B on 1 June. On 8 June B sells them onto C. On 10 June, it is discovered that B had made a misrepresentation in the original contract between A and B and A seeks to recover the goods. Given these dates, A cannot do so, as the goods have been sold on to C *before* A tries to avoid the original contract, and at the time that B sells them he (B) still has good title.

If on the other hand, B did not sell the goods on to C until 12 June, which is after A seeks to avoid the original contract with B, that original contract has already been avoided, and B would not be able to pass good title on to C.

(c) An **unenforceable contract** is a **valid contract** and property transferred under it cannot be recovered even from the other party to the contract. If either party refuses to perform the contract, the other party cannot compel him to do so. A contract is usually unenforceable when the required evidence of its terms, for example, written evidence of a contract relating to land, is not available. Unenforceable contracts are only problematic if a dispute over the contract arises.

The life of a contract

Once a valid contract has been formed, it remains in existence until **discharged,** usually in one of four ways. The most common means of discharge is **performance**, where both parties fulfil their contractual obligations. The most common problem arises where there is a **breach of contract,** whereby one party fails to carry out their side of the contract properly.

NOTES

Chapter roundup

- The three essential components of a contract are offer and acceptance, consideration and the intention of the parties to create legal relations

- A void contract is one which has no legal effect at any time: neither party can obtain rights or obligations under it

- A voidable contract is one which is valid unless and until it is avoided

- An unenforceable contract is one which is valid but which cannot be enforced by either of the parties should something go wrong

Quick quiz

1   What is a standard form contract?

2   What are the three essentials of a valid contract?

3   Define void, voidable and unenforceable contracts.

Answers to quick quiz

1   Contract produced by large companies setting its own compulsory terms.

2   - Intention to create legal relations
    - Offer and acceptance
    - Consideration

3   (a)   A **void** contract is **not a contract** at all. The parties are not bound by it and if they transfer property under it they can sometimes (unless it is also an illegal contract) recover their goods even from a third party.

    (b)   A **voidable** contract is a **contract which one party may avoid**, that is terminate at his option. The contract is treated as valid unless and until it is avoided. Property transferred before avoidance is usually irrecoverable from a third party.

    (c)   An **unenforceable** contract is a **valid contract** and property transferred under it cannot be recovered even from the other party to the contract. If either party refuses to perform the contract, the other party cannot compel him to do so. A contract is usually unenforceable when the required evidence of its terms, for example, written evidence of a contract relating to land, is not available. Unenforceable contracts are only problematic if a dispute over the contract arises.

Assignment

Since the content of this chapter is introductory reading and it will be developed in the following chapters, we do not include a specific assignment for this chapter.

However, remember that you will encounter many of the terms and concepts here in the following chapters, and you may be expected to apply them in assignments at that stage.

Chapter 4 :
AGREEMENT

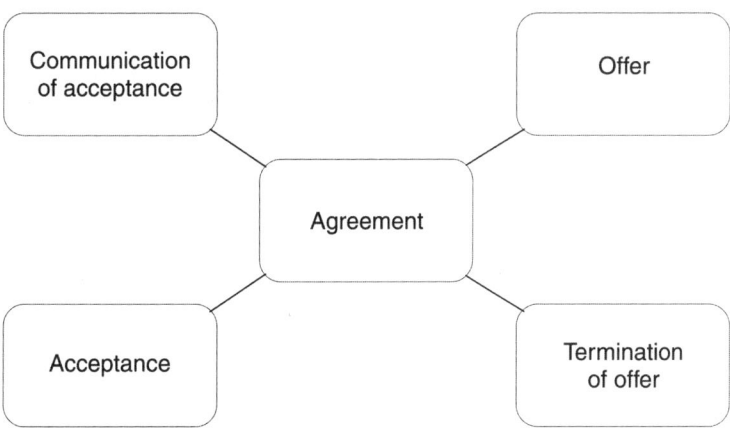

Introduction

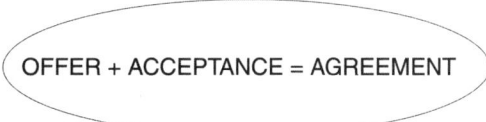

OFFER + ACCEPTANCE = AGREEMENT

The first essential element of a binding contract is **agreement**. To determine whether or not an agreement has been reached, the courts will consider whether one party has made a firm offer which the other party has accepted.

In most contracts, **offer and acceptance** may be made orally or in writing, or they may be implied by the conduct of the parties. The person making an offer is the **offeror** and the person to whom an offer is made is the **offeree**.

The **particular significance of offer and acceptance is that a binding contract is thereby formed**, so that new terms cannot thereafter be introduced into the contract unless both parties agree. From this moment on, the terms of the contract appear from the offer and acceptance, rather than from the unexpressed intentions of the parties.

Your objectives

In this chapter you will learn about the following.

(a)   What 'an offer' is in law

(b)   How it is distinguished from other things

(c)   What 'acceptance' is in law

(d)   How it is distinguished from other things

(e)   How acceptance must be communicated to create agreement

NOTES

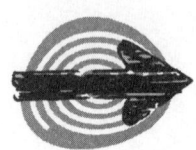

Note. This is the first chapter in which you have seen detailed references to cases. They are usually presented with the claimant's (or plaintiff's) name first, and then the name of the defendant. The names may sometimes be reversed where the case has gone to appeal and the original defendant is now bringing the appeal.

1 OFFER

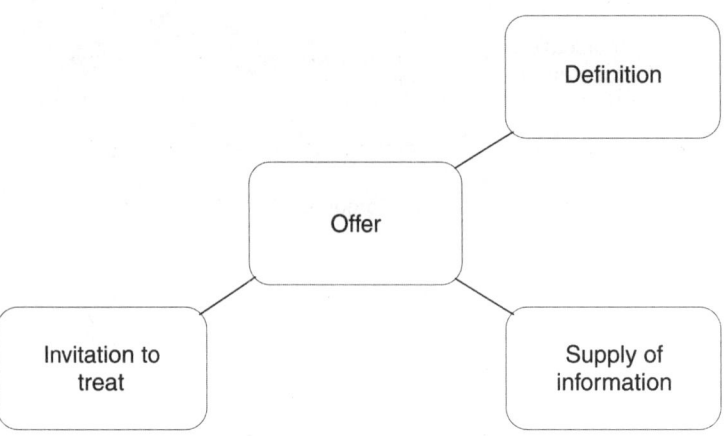

1.1 Definition

> An **offer** is a definite promise to be bound on specific terms.

Certainty of the offer

An apparently vague offer can be made certain by reference to the parties' previous dealing.

> *Gunthing v Lynn 1831*
> *The facts*: the offeror offered to pay a further sum for a horse if it was 'lucky'.
>
> *Decision*: the offer was too vague and no contract could be formed by any purported acceptance.
>
> *Hillas & Co Ltd v Arcos Ltd 1932*
> *The facts*: the claimants agreed to purchase from the defendants '22,000 standards of softwood goods of fair specification over the season 1930'. The agreement contained an option to buy a further 100,000 standards in 1931. The 1930 transaction took place but the sellers refused to supply any wood in 1931, saying that the agreement was too vague to bind the parties.
>
> *Decision:* the wording used, and the previous transactions, showed a sufficient intention to be bound. There was therefore a valid contract.

A definite offer may be made to a **class** of persons or to **the world at large**.

> *Carlill v Carbolic Smoke Ball Co 1893*
> *The facts*: the manufacturers of a patent medicine published an advertisement by which they undertook to pay '£100 reward ... to any person who contracts

... influenza ... after having used the smoke ball three times daily for two weeks'. The advertisement added that £1,000 had been deposited at a bank 'showing our sincerity in this matter'. The claimant read the advertisement, purchased the smoke ball and used it as directed. She contracted influenza and claimed her £100 reward. The manufacturers argued a number of defences, including the following.

(a) The offer was so vague that it could not form the basis of a contract as no time limit was specified.

(b) It was not an offer which could be accepted since it was offered to the whole world.

Decision: the court considered these two defences as follows.

(a) The smoke ball must protect the user during the period of use. The offer was not vague.

(b) An offer to the public can be accepted so as to form a contract.

1.2 Supply of information

Only an offer in the proper sense may be accepted so as to form a binding contract. The supply of information will not be considered to be an offer.

> *Harvey v Facey 1893*
> *The facts*: the claimant telegraphed to the defendant 'Will you sell us Bumper Hall Pen? Telegraph lowest cash price'. The defendant telegraphed in reply 'Lowest price for Bumper Hall Pen, £900'. The claimant telegraphed to accept what he regarded as an offer; the defendant made no further reply.
>
> *Decision*: the defendant's telegram was merely a statement of his minimum price if a sale were to be agreed. It was not an offer and no contract had been made.

If, in the course of negotiations for a sale, the vendor states the price at which he will sell, that statement may be an offer which can become accepted eventually.

> *Bigg v Boyd Gibbons 1971*
> *The facts*: in the course of correspondence the defendant rejected an offer of £20,000 by the claimant and added 'for a quick sale I would accept £26,000 .... if you are not interested in this price would you please let me know immediately'. The claimant accepted this price of £26,000 and the defendant acknowledged his acceptance, stating that he had given instructions for the sale to his solicitor.
>
> *Decision*: in this context the defendant must be treated as making an offer (at £26,000) which the claimant had accepted.

A statement of intention

Advertising that an event such as an auction will take place is not an offer to sell. Potential buyers may not sue if the auction does not take place: *Harris v Nickerson 1873*

NOTES

1.3 An invitation to treat

Where a party is initiating negotiations, he is said to have made an invitation to treat.

Definition

> An **invitation to treat** is an indication that someone is prepared to receive offers with the view to forming a binding contract. It is not an offer in itself.

There are four types of invitation to treat.

- Auction sales
- Advertisements
- Exhibition of goods for sale
- An invitation for tenders

Auction sales

An auctioneer's request for bids is not a definite offer to sell to the highest bidder. The bid itself is the offer, which the auctioneer is then free to accept or reject: *Payne v Cave 1789*. Acceptance is indicated by the fall of the auctioneer's hammer.

Advertisements

An advertisement of goods is an attempt to induce offers and is therefore classified as an invitation to treat.

> *Partridge v Crittenden 1968*
>
> *The facts*: Mr Partridge placed an advertisement in *Cage and Aviary Birds* magazine containing the words 'Bramblefinch cocks, bramblefinch hens, 25s each'. The RSPCA brought a prosecution for offering for sale a protected species in contravention of the Protection of Birds Act 1953. The justices convicted Partridge. He appealed to the Court of Appeal.
>
> *Decision*: the conviction was quashed. The prosecution could not rely on the offence of 'offering for sale', as the advertisement constituted an invitation to treat. He was therefore not making an offer.

The circulation of a price list is also an invitation to treat: *Grainger v Gough 1896*. It cannot be an offer because 'if it were so, the merchant might find himself involved in any number of contractual obligations to supply wine of a particular description which he would be quite unable to carry out, his stock of wine of that description being necessarily limited.'

Activity 1 **(2 mins)**

In *Carlill v Carbolic Smokeball Co 1893*, the company published an advertisement for its patent medicine in which it undertook to pay £100 to anyone who, having used the medicine, became ill with influenza within a limited period thereafter.

At what time was the contract between Mrs Carlill and the company made?

A   When she read the advertisement
B   When she bought the patent medicine
C   When she used the medicine and caught influenza
D   When she notified the manufacturer of her claim

Exhibition of goods for sale

Displaying goods in a shop constitutes inviting customers to make offers to purchase, or an invitation to treat.

> *Fisher v Bell 1961*
> *The facts*: a shopkeeper was prosecuted for offering for sale an offensive weapon by exhibiting a flick knife in his shop window.
>
> *Decision*: according to the ordinary law of contract, the display of an article with a price on it in a shop window is merely an invitation to treat. Therefore he was not offering the knife for sale, but rather inviting offers from potential purchasers. The shop keeper would then be able to either accept or reject the offer.

> *Pharmaceutical Society of Great Britain v Boots Cash Chemists (Southern) 1952*
> *The facts*: certain drugs containing poisons could only be sold 'under the supervision of a registered pharmacist'. The claimant claimed this rule had been broken by Boots who put supplies of these drugs on open shelves in a self-service shop. Boots contended that there was no sale until the customer brought the goods to the cash desk and offered to buy them. A registered pharmacist was stationed at this point.
>
> *Decision*: The court found for the defendant (Boots) and commented that if it were true that a customer accepted an offer to sell by removing goods from the shelf he could not then change his mind and put them back because to do so would constitute breach of contract.

Invitation for tenders

A tender is an estimate submitted in response to a prior request. When a person tenders for a contract he is making an offer to the person who has advertised a contract as being available. If you want an extension built on your house, you might obtain tenders from three different builders. You therefore receive three offers and you decide which one to accept.

NOTES

Activity 2 (10 mins)

Bianca goes into a shop and sees a price label on a CD for £15. She takes the CD to the checkout, but the till operator tells her that the label is misprinted and should read £20. Bianca maintains that she only has to pay £15. How would you describe the price on the price label in terms of contract law?

FOR DISCUSSION

As seen in the *Partridge v Crittenden* case, the general rule is that an advertisement will not be interpreted as an offer. However, in *Carlill's case* the advertisement by the Carbolic Smoke Ball Co was construed as an offer that could be accepted by Mrs Carlill's act. What factors do you think a judge would consider relevant in determining whether an offer has been made?

2   TERMINATION OF OFFER

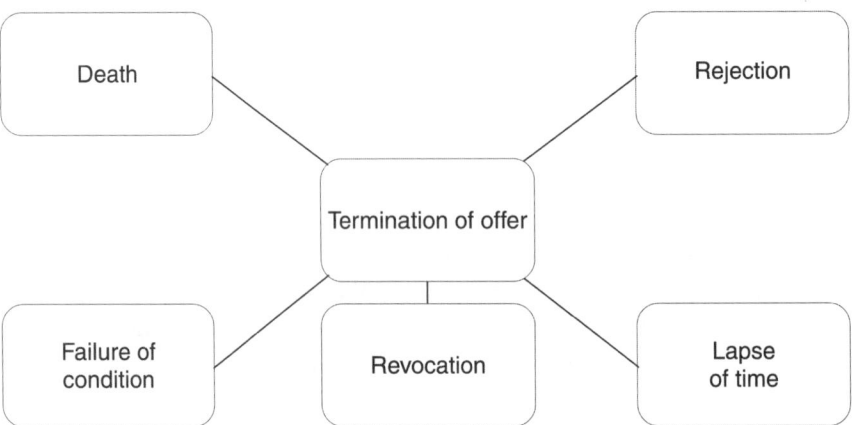

The key way that an offer is terminated is by being accepted, thereby creating agreement. An offer is **terminated** so that it may no longer be accepted in any of the following circumstances.

- Rejection
- Lapse of time
- Revocation by the offeror
- Failure of a condition to which the offer was subject
- Death of one of the parties

PROFESSIONAL EDUCATION

2.1 Rejection

Outright rejection terminates an offer. A counter-offer also terminates the original offer.

> *Hyde v Wrench 1840*
> *The facts:* W offered to sell his farm for £1,000. H offered £950 (a counter-offer) which W rejected. A few days later H said he would buy for £1,000. W refused to sell and H maintained that they had a contract.
>
> *Decision:* the counter-offer of £950 had rejected the original offer to sell of £1,000.

2.2 Lapse of time

An offer may be expressed to last for a **specified time**. If there is no express time limit set, it expires after a **reasonable time.** What is reasonable depends on the circumstances of the case.

> *Ramsgate Victoria Hotel Co v Montefiore 1866*
> *The facts*: the defendant applied to the company in June for shares and paid a deposit to the company's bank. At the end of November the company sent him an acceptance by issue of a letter of allotment and requested payment of the balance due. The defendant contended that his offer had expired and could no longer be accepted.
>
> *Decision*: the offer was for a reasonable time only, so the offer had lapsed.

2.3 Revocation by the offeror

The offeror may revoke his offer at any time before acceptance: *Payne v Cave 1789*.

If he undertakes that his offer shall remain open for acceptance for a specified time he may nonetheless revoke it within that time, unless by a separate contract he has bound himself to keep it open for the whole of the specified time.

> *Routledge v Grant 1828*
> *The facts*: the defendant offered to buy the claimant's house for a fixed sum, requiring acceptance within six weeks. Within the six weeks specified, he withdrew his offer.
>
> *Decision*: the defendant could revoke his offer at any time before acceptance, even though the time limit had not expired.

Revocation may be an express statement to that effect or may be an act of the offeror indicating that he no longer regards the offer as in force. His revocation does not take effect **until the revocation is communicated to the offeree**. This raises two important points.

While posting a letter is a sufficient act of acceptance (as we shall see shortly), it is not a sufficient act of revocation of offer.

> *Byrne v Van Tienhoven 1880*
> *The facts*: the defendants were in Cardiff; the claimants in New York. The sequence of events was as follows:
> 1 October Letter posted in Cardiff, offering to sell 1,000 boxes of tinplates.
> 8 October Letter of revocation of offer posted in Cardiff.

11 October   Letter of offer received in New York and telegram of acceptance sent.

15 October   Letter confirming acceptance posted in New York.

20 October   Letter of revocation received in New York. The offeree had meanwhile resold the contract goods.

Decision: the letter of revocation could not take effect until received (20 October). Simply posting a letter does not revoke the offer until it is received. Therefore there was a binding contract.

While acceptance must be communicated by the offeree, revocation of offer may be communicated by any third party who is a sufficiently reliable informant.

Dickinson v Dodds 1876

The facts: the defendant, on 10 June, wrote to the claimant to offer property for sale at £800, adding 'this offer to be left open until Friday 12 June, 9.00 am'. On 11 June the defendant sold the property to another buyer. The intermediary between Dickinson and Dodds informed Dickinson that the defendant had sold to someone else. On Friday 12 June, before 9.00 am, the claimant handed to the defendant a formal letter of acceptance.

Decision: the defendant was free to revoke his offer and had done so by sale to a third party; the claimant could not accept the offer after he had learnt from a reliable informant of the revocation of the offer to him.

Where an offer is meant to be accepted by conduct (a **unilateral** contract), it has been held that it cannot be revoked once the offeree has begun to try and perform whatever act is necessary.

Errington v Errington 1953

The facts: a father bought a house for his son and daughter-in-law to live in. He paid the deposit, and the son and daughter-in-law were to make the mortgage repayments. The father told them that the house would be theirs when the mortgage was paid off. The son subsequently left his wife, who continued to live in the house.

Decision: The Court of Appeal ruled that the father could not eject the daughter-in-law from the property. Lord Denning said 'The father's promise was a unilateral contract – a promise of the house in return for their act of paying the instalments. It could not be revoked by him once the couple entered on the performance of the act ...'.

2.4   Failure of a condition

An offer may be conditional. If the condition is not satisfied, the offer is not capable of acceptance.

Financings Ltd v Stimson 1962

The facts: the defendant wished to purchase a car, and on 16 March signed a hire-purchase form. The form, issued by the claimants, stated that the agreement would be binding only upon signature by them. On 20 March the defendant, not satisfied with the car, returned it to the motor dealer. On 24 March the car was stolen from the premises of the dealer, and was recovered

badly damaged. On 25 March the claimants signed the form. They sued the defendant for breach of contract.

Decision: the defendant was not bound to take the car. His signing of the agreement was actually an offer to contract with the claimant. There was an implied condition in this offer that the car would be in substantially the same condition when the offer was accepted as when it was made.

2.5 Termination by death

The death of the **offeree** terminates the offer.

The **offeror's** death terminates the offer unless the offeree accepts it in ignorance of the offeror's death, and the offer is not of a personal nature.

3 ACCEPTANCE

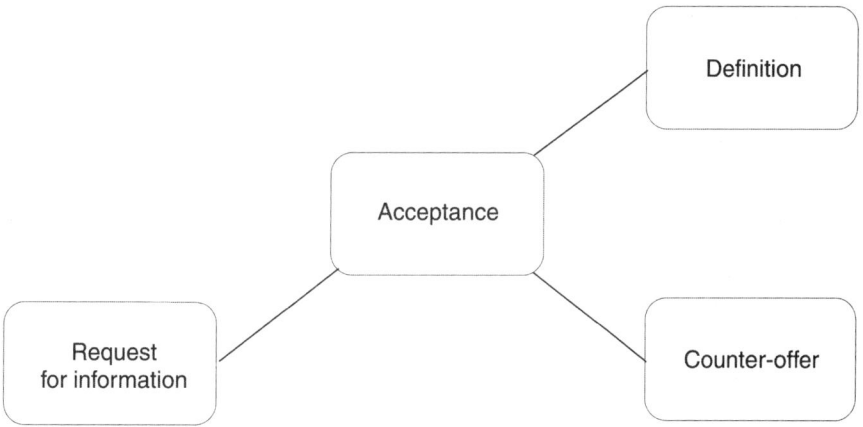

3.1 Definition

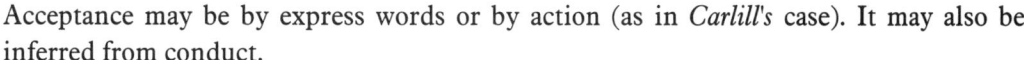

Acceptance is the unqualified agreement to the terms of the offer.

Acceptance may be by express words or by action (as in *Carlill's* case). It may also be inferred from conduct.

> *Brogden v Metropolitan Railway Co 1877*
> *The facts*: having supplied coal for many years to the defendant, the claimant suggested there should be a written agreement. The claimant continued to supply coal under the terms of the draft agreement but no version was ever signed. The claimant later denied that there was any agreement between him and the defendant.
>
> *Decision*: the conduct of the parties indicated that they both agreed to the terms of the draft. The draft agreement became a binding contract as soon as the defendant ordered and the claimant supplied coal.

Silence as acceptance

There must be some act on the part of the offeree to indicate his acceptance.

> *Felthouse v Bindley 1862*
> *The facts*: the claimant wrote to his nephew offering to buy the nephew's horse for £30.15s, adding 'If I hear no more about him, I consider the horse mine at that price'. The nephew intended to accept his uncle's offer but did not reply. He instructed the defendant, an auctioneer, not to sell the horse. Owing to a misunderstanding the horse was sold at auction to someone else. The uncle sued the auctioneer in conversion (a tort alleging wrongful disposal of another's property).
>
> *Decision*: the action failed. There could be no acceptance by silence in these circumstances. The claimant had no title to the horse and could not sue in conversion.

Unsolicited goods

Goods which are sent or services which are rendered to a person who did not request them are not 'accepted' merely because he does not return them to the sender. His silence is not acceptance of them, even if the sender includes a statement that he is deemed to have agreed to buy and/or pay unless he rejects them: Unsolicited Goods and Services Act 1971.

3.2 Counter-offer

As has been said, acceptance must be unqualified agreement to the terms of the offer. **Acceptance which purports to introduce any new terms is a counter-offer**. If a counter-offer is made, the original offeror may accept it, but if he rejects it his original offer is no longer available for acceptance. Refer back to the case *Hyde v Wrench* in paragraph 2.1 for an example of a counter-offer.

A counter-offer may be accepted by the original offeror; this will have the effect of creating a binding contract.

> *Butler Machine Tool Co v Ex-cell-O Corp (England) 1979*
> *The facts:* the claimant offered to sell tools to the defendant. Their quotation included details of their standard terms and conditions of sale. The defendant 'accepted' the offer, enclosing their own standard terms, which differed from those of the claimant. The claimant acknowledged acceptance by returning a tear-off slip from the order form.
>
> *Decision*: the defendant's order was really a counter-offer. The claimant had accepted this by returning the tear-off slip.

Activity 3 (5 mins)

Mike offered to sell Barry his car for £5,000. Barry agreed but said he would pay by five instalments of £1,000 per month. Mike then sold the car to Catherine. Barry plans to sue Mike for breach of contract. Will he succeed?

3.3 Request for information

It is possible, however, to respond to an offer by making a **request for information**.

> *Stevenson v McLean 1880*
>
> *The facts*: the defendant offered to sell iron at '40s per ton, open till Monday'. The claimant replied asking about delivery times, and then sent a letter accepting the offer. This crossed in the post with a letter from the defendant which revoked the offer. The defendant sold the iron to a third party.
>
> *Decision*: there was a contract since the claimant had merely enquired as to a variation of terms. The offer was still open when it was accepted by the claimant.

4 COMMUNICATION OF ACCEPTANCE

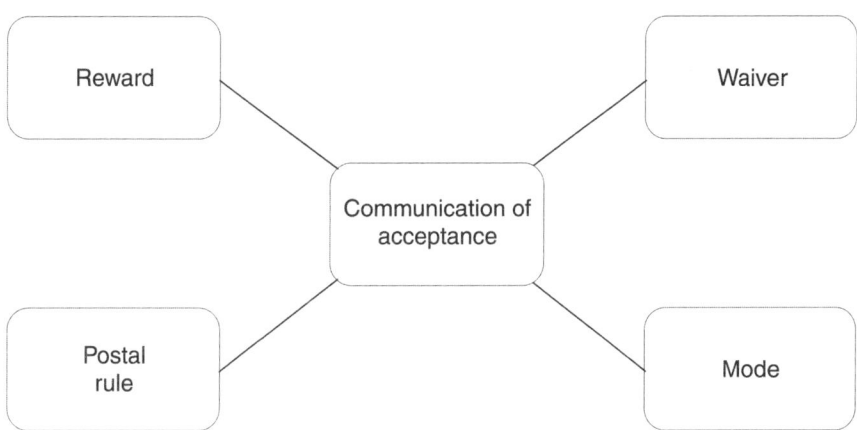

The general rule is that acceptance must be **communicated** to the offeror and is **not effective until this has been done.**

4.1 Waiver of communication

The offeror may, by his offer, dispense with the need for communication of acceptance. In *Carlill v Carbolic Smoke Ball Co 1893*, it was held that it was sufficient for the claimant to act on the offer without previously notifying her acceptance of it. This was an example of a **unilateral contract,** where the offer takes the form of a promise to pay money in return for an act.

4.2 Prescribed mode of communication

The offeror may call for acceptance by specified means. Unless he stipulates that this is the only method of acceptance which suffices, then acceptance by some other means equally expeditious would constitute a valid acceptance: *Tinn v Hoffmann 1873*. A telegram or even a verbal message could be sufficient acceptance of an offer inviting acceptance 'by return of post'. This would probably apply now also to acceptance by fax machine or e-mail.

Yates Building Co v R J Pulleyn & Sons (York) 1975
The facts: the offer called for acceptance by registered or recorded delivery letter. The offeree sent an ordinary letter which arrived without delay, at the same time as a registered or recorded delivery letter would have arrived.

Decision: the offeror had suffered no disadvantage and had not stipulated that acceptance must be made in this way only. The acceptance was valid.

4.3 The postal rule

The offeror may expressly or by implication indicate that he expects acceptance by means of a letter sent through the post. The **postal rule** states that, where the use of the post is within the contemplation of **both** the parties, the acceptance is complete and effective as soon as a letter is **posted**.

Adams v Lindsell 1818
The facts: the defendants made an offer by letter to the claimant on 2 September 1817 requiring an answer 'in course of post'. The letter of offer was delayed and reached the claimants on 5 September; they immediately posted a letter of acceptance, which reached the defendants on 9 September. The defendants could have expected a reply by 7 September, and they assumed that the absence of a reply within the expected period indicated non-acceptance and sold the goods to another buyer on 8 September.

Decision: the acceptance was made 'in course of post' and was effective when posted. The contract was made on 5 September, when the acceptance was posted.

The intention to use the post for communication of acceptance may be deduced from the circumstances without express statement to that effect.

Household Fire and Carriage Accident Insurance Co v Grant 1879
The facts: the defendant handed a letter of application for shares to the claimant company's agent in Swansea with the intention that it should be posted to the company in London. The company posted an acceptance (letter of allotment) which was lost in the post, and never arrived. The defendant was called upon to pay the amount outstanding on his shares.

Decision: the defendant had to pay. The contract between the company and him had been formed when the letter of allotment was posted, regardless of the fact that it was lost in the post.

Under the postal rule, the offeror may be unaware that a contract has been made by acceptance of his offer. If that possibility is clearly inconsistent with the nature of the transaction, the postal rule is excluded and the letter of acceptance takes effect only when received.

Holwell Securities v Hughes 1974
The facts: Hughes granted to the claimant an option to purchase land to be exercised 'by notice in writing'. A letter giving notice of the exercise of the option was lost in the post.

Decision: the words 'notice in writing' must mean notice actually received by the vendor; hence notice had not been given to accept the offer.

Acceptance of an offer may only be made by a person authorised to do so. This will usually be the offeree or his authorised agents.

> *Powell v Lee 1908*
> *The facts*: the claimant successfully applied for a post as a headmaster. Without authorisation, the claimant was informed of the appointment by one of the managers. Later, it was decided to give the post to someone else. The claimant sued for breach of contract.
>
> *Decision*: he failed in his action for breach of contract. Since communication of acceptance was unauthorised, there was no valid agreement and hence no contract.

Activity 4   **(10 mins)**

Jarvis wrote to Cocker on 1 April offering to sell him his mountain bike for £2,000, and asking Cocker to reply by post. Cocker received the letter on 2 April and the same day posted a letter of acceptance. On 3 April, Jarvis telephoned Cocker to say he was increasing the price to £2,500, but Cocker is insisting on buying at £2,000. What is the legal position?

4.4 Reward cases

The question arises as to whether contractual obligations arise if a party, in ignorance of an offer, performs an act which fulfils the terms of the offer. If A offers a reward to anyone who finds and returns his lost property and B, in ignorance of the offer, does in fact return it to him, is B entitled to the promised reward? In fact there is no contract by which A is obliged to pay the reward to B.

> *R v Clarke 1927*
> *The facts*: a reward of £1,000 was offered for information leading to the arrest and conviction of a murderer. C, an accomplice, gave the necessary information. He claimed the reward, admitting that he had acted only to save his own skin.
>
> *Decision*: his claim failed. Although he had seen the offer, it was not present in his mind when he acted.

However, acceptance may still be valid even if the offer was not the sole reason for the action.

NOTES

Chapter roundup

- The first essential element of a binding contract is agreement. This is usually evidenced by offer and acceptance.

- An offer is a definite promise to be bound on specific terms, and must be distinguished from the mere supply of information and from an invitation to treat.

- An offer is terminated, and no longer open for acceptance, in the following circumstances.

  ○ Rejection by the offeree
  ○ Lapse of time
  ○ Revocation by the offeror
  ○ Failure of a condition to which the offer was subject
  ○ Death of one of the parties.

- Acceptance must be unqualified agreement to all the terms of the offer. It may be by express words or inferred from conduct. Inaction does not imply acceptance.

- A counter-offer is a rejection of the original offer.

- Acceptance is not effective until communicated to the offeror, with two exceptions.

  ○ The offeror may waive the need for communication of acceptance by making an offer to the entire world.

  ○ He may indicate that he expects acceptance through the post.

- In the latter case, the 'postal rule' applies: acceptance is complete and effective as soon as notice of it is posted.

Quick quiz

1   What case illustrates the principle that an offer may be made to the world at large?

2   What is an invitation to treat?

3   Can a third party communicate revocation of an offer?

4   What happens when an offeree accepts an offer but applies different terms to it?

5   What does the postal rule say?

Answers to quick quiz

1   Carlill v Carbolic Smokeball Co. 1893.

2   An indication that someone is prepared to receive offers.

3   Yes, as long as he is reliable.

4   A new offer is created which can be either accepted or rejected.

5   The acceptance is effective as seen as it is posted, as long as the post is the expected means of communication.

Answers to activities

1   When she used the medicine and caught influenza. This was acceptance of the offer which, because it was to the entire world, had dispensed with the need for communication of acceptance. The answer is C.

2   A price label is an invitation to treat (*Fisher v Bell 1961*) ie an invitation to the customer to make an offer which the shop can either accept or reject.

3   No. By introducing the payment terms, Barry has rejected Mike's original offer and made a counter-offer to buy the car for £5,000 but pay over five months. Mike is free to accept or reject this, and by selling to Catherine, rejects Barry's offer.

4   Cocker can enforce the contract. The post is seen as the means of acceptance and, following the postal rule, Cocker has accepted. There is a contract.

Assignment 1   **(45 mins)**

Adam is a secondhand car dealer. He places an advertisement in the Saturday edition of his local paper stating:

'Once in a lifetime opportunity: a one year old, low mileage, Mota Special: £5,000 cash. This is a serious offer – the car will go to the first person who accepts it – valid for one day only.'

When Ben sees the advert he immediately posts a letter of acceptance of Adam's offer.

Carol also sees the advert and after inspecting the car offers Adam a cheque for £5,000, but he refuses to accept the cheque and tells her she cannot have the car.

Later in the day Dave asks Adam if he will keep the offer open until he can get to his bank to arrange a loan. Adam agrees but later in the day when Eric says that he will pay £6,000 in cash for the car he agrees to sell the car to Eric.

On Monday morning Ben's letter arrives, and Dave returns to complete his purchase of the car. In the afternoon Eric phones Adam to say that he has had second thoughts and no longer wishes to buy the car.

Required

Consider the above situation with respect to the rules governing the creation of contracts.

In particular consider:

(a)   The precise nature of Adam's advertisement
(b)   Whether Ben has entered into a binding contract with Adam
(c)   Whether Carol has any right of action against Adam
(d)   Whether Dave has any right of action against Adam
(e)   Whether Adam has any right of action against Eric

Chapter 5 :
CONSIDERATION

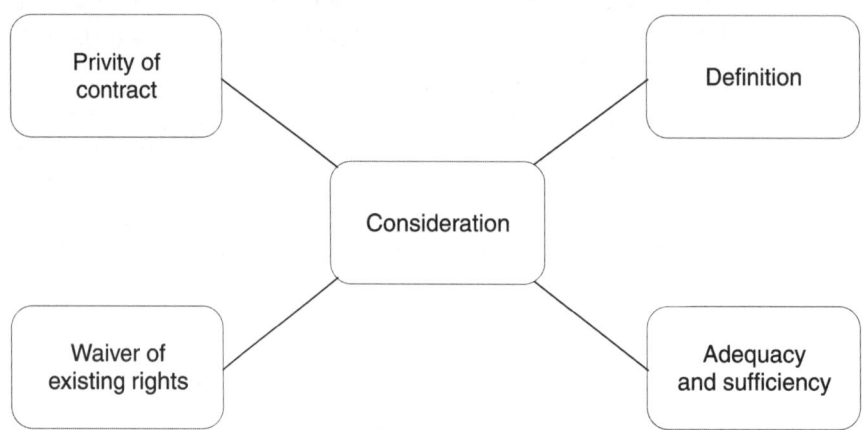

Introduction

Consideration is also one of the three essential elements of a binding contract. The principle is that the parties to a contract must each provide something, whether money, the provision of a service or some other form of contribution to the contract. A contractual promise is one which is not purely gratuitous. If a window cleaner telephones you and promises as a special promotion to clean your windows tomorrow for free, but then fails to turn up, you cannot sue him for breach of contract. This is because there is no contract, because you have provided no consideration.

Your objectives

In this chapter you will learn about the following.

    (a)   The nature of consideration

    (b)   The rules governing past consideration

    (c)   The rules governing adequacy of consideration

    (d)   The rules governing sufficiency of consideration

    (e)   The rules governing the doctrine of promissory estoppel

    (f)   The rule of privity of contract

1 DEFINITION

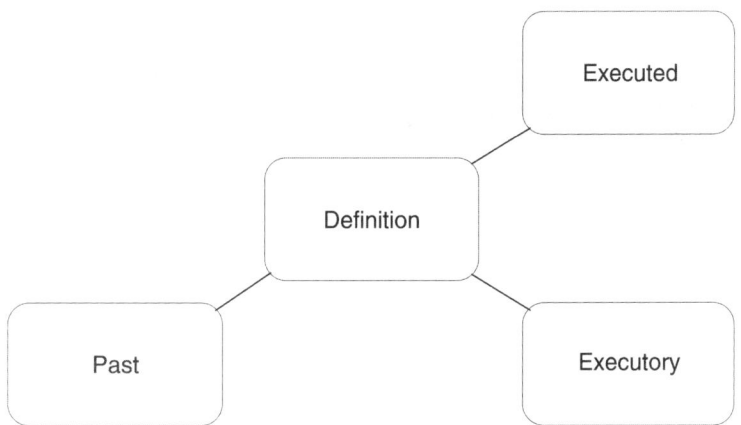

There have been a number of case law definitions of consideration, for example from *Currie v Misa 1875*

Definitions

> 'A valuable **consideration** in the sense of the law may consist either in some right, interest, profit or benefit accruing to one party, or some forbearance, detriment, loss or responsibility given, suffered or undertaken by the other.'

Using the language of purchase and sale, it could be said that one party must know that he has bought the other party's promises either by performing some **act** of his own or by offering a **promise** of his own. Consideration has also been described as 'the price of the other person's promise'.

There are a very few situation when consideration is not required. One of these is a **specialty contract**.

Definition

> A **specialty contract** is one where consideration is not a compulsory element. An example is the granting of a deed, such as a deed of covenant in favour of a charity. The charity does not have to provide any consideration in return.
>
> This is in contrast to a **simple contract** (most types of contract) which is one where consideration is provided by both sides.

It is sometimes said that valid consideration may be **executed** or **executory**, but it **cannot be past**. These terms are explained below.

NOTES

1.1 Executed consideration

Definition

> **Executed consideration** is a performed, or executed, act in return for a promise.

If, for example, A offers a reward for the return of lost property, his promise becomes binding when B performs the act of returning A's property to him. The claimant's act in Carlill's case in response to the smoke ball company's promise of reward was thus executed consideration.

1.2 Executory consideration

Definition

> **Executory consideration** is a promise given for a promise, not a performed act.

If, for example, a customer orders goods which a shopkeeper undertakes to obtain from the manufacturer, the shopkeeper promises to supply the goods and the customer promises to accept and pay for them. It would be breach of contract if either withdrew without the consent of the other.

1.3 Past consideration

Both executed and executory consideration are provided at the time when the promise is given.

Definition

> Anything which has already been done before a promise in return is given is **past consideration** which, as a general rule, is not sufficient to make the promise binding.

Re McArdle 1951

The facts: under the terms of a will, children were entitled to a house after their mother's death. In the mother's lifetime one of the sons and his wife lived in the house with the mother. The wife made improvements to the house. The children later agreed in writing to repay to the wife the sum of £488 'in consideration of your carrying out certain alterations and improvements' to the property. At the mother's death they refused to do so.

Decision: the work on the house had been completed before the documents were signed. At the time of the promise the improvements were past consideration.

If there is an existing contract and one party makes a further promise, no contract will arise.

> *Roscorla v Thomas 1842*
>
> *The facts*: the claimant agreed to buy a horse from the defendant at a given price. When negotiations were over and the contract was formed, the defendant told the claimant that the horse was 'sound and free from vice'. The horse turned out to be vicious and the claimant brought an action on the warranty.
>
> *Decision*: the express promise was made after the sale was over and was unsupported by fresh consideration.

Exceptions to the doctrine of past consideration

In three cases past consideration for a promise can make the promise binding.

(a)   Past consideration is sufficient to create liability on a **bill of exchange** (such as a cheque) under s 27 Bills of Exchange Act 1882.

(b)   After six (or in some cases twelve) years the right to sue for recovery of a debt becomes statute barred by the **Limitation Act 1980**. If, after that period, the debtor makes written acknowledgement of the creditor's claim, the claim is again enforceable at law. The debt, although past consideration, suffices.

(c)   When a request is made for a service this **request may imply a promise** to pay for it. If, after the service has been rendered, the person who made the request promises a specific reward, this is treated as fixing the amount to be paid under the previous implied promise.

> *Lampleigh v Braithwait 1615*
>
> *The facts*: the defendant had killed a man and had asked the claimant to obtain for him a royal pardon. The claimant did so, 'riding and journeying to and from London and Newmarket' at his own expense. The defendant then promised to pay him £100. He failed to pay it and was sued.
>
> *Decision*: the defendant's request was regarded as containing an implied promise to pay, and the subsequent promise merely fixed the amount.

The third exception above has been somewhat revised by the courts, so that both parties must have assumed throughout their negotiations that the services were ultimately to be paid for.

> *Re Casey's Patents 1892*
>
> *The facts*: A and B, joint owners of patent rights, asked their employee, C, as an extra task to find licensees to work the patents. After C had done so, A and B agreed to reward him for his past services with one third of the patent rights. A died and his executors denied that the promise made was binding.
>
> *Decision*: the promise to C was binding since it fixed the 'reasonable remuneration' which A and B by implication promised to pay before the service was given.

> ### Activity 1 (10 mins)
>
> Which of the following is valid consideration? Try to state the law to justify your answer.
>
> (a) An action six months ago for which the person who carried it out is now demanding payment.
>
> (b) A promise to pay for goods in six months time.
>
> (c) A request to someone to clean your windows.

2 ADEQUACY AND SUFFICIENCY

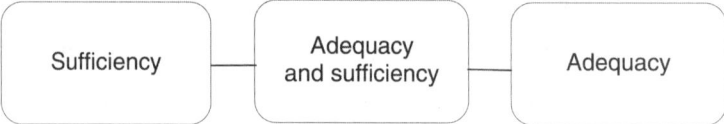

The law says that consideration need not be adequate but it must be sufficient. This means that the consideration need not be of equal value to the parties to the contract, but it must be of some value to the parties involved. This does not have to be financial or monetary value, although obviously in many contracts it often is.

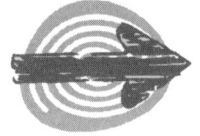

In a basic contract for the sale of goods, one party will provide money as his consideration, and the other party will provide the goods.

2.1 Adequacy

> *Chappell & Co v Nestle Co Ltd*
>
> *The facts*: The defendants made a special offer, whereby if people collected three wrappers from Nestle bars of chocolate and then sent them in with a small sum of money, they could get a copy of a record called 'Rockin' Shoes'. The case arose because the claimants owned the copyright to the music and the two parties were trying to calculate the amount of royalties payable to Chappell, on the basis of the value of the records. The argument hinged on whether the wrappers, which were merely thrown away on receipt by Nestle, constituted part of the consideration and therefore should be included in the royalty calculation.
>
> *Decision*: The defendants had required that wrappers were sent in as part of the special offer, for obvious commercial reasons. It was held that the wrappers were part of the consideration as they had commercial value in the eyes of Nestle, one of the parties to the contract.

No protection against a bad bargain

The courts have always made it clear that parties to a contract are expected to look after themselves, and the courts will not protect them if all they have done is made a 'bad bargain' and accepted inadequate consideration. Therefore, if someone sells their car,

worth £10,000, for £2,000, they cannot expect the courts to step in, unless there has been some element of fraud or misrepresentation in the run up to the contract.

The courts will not seek to weigh up the comparative values of the promises.

> *Thomas v Thomas 1842*
> *The facts*: by his will the claimant's husband expressed the wish that his widow should have the use of his house during her life. The defendants allowed the widow to occupy the house (a) in accordance with her husband's wishes and (b) in return for her undertaking to pay a rent of £1 per annum. They later said that their promise to let her occupy the house was not supported by consideration.
>
> *Decision*: compliance with the husband's wishes was not valuable consideration (because there was no economic value attached to it), but the nominal rent was sufficient consideration, even though inadequate as a rent.

The value of forbearance

Forbearance, or the promise to give something up or to stop doing something, can be adequate consideration, if it has some value or amounts to giving up something of value. For example, a contract in which one party promises to give up smoking would probably have adequate consideration.

However, although consideration need not be adequate it must be **sufficient**.

2.2 Sufficiency

The term **sufficiency of consideration** means that the consideration must be something more than the party involved was already intended to do. It must be deemed actually to be consideration. For example the performance of an existing legal duty cannot be regarded as consideration, as the person involved would be going to do it anyway.

Performance of existing contractual duties

Performance of an **existing obligation** imposed by statute is **no consideration** for a promise of reward.

> *Collins v Godefroy 1831*
> *The facts*: the claimant had been subpoenaed (ie summoned to court) to give evidence on behalf of the defendant in another case. He alleged that the defendant had promised to pay him six guineas (£6.30) for appearing.
>
> *Decision*: there was no consideration for this promise, as the claimant was obliged to appear by law. He failed in his claim for the six guineas.

But if some extra service is given, that is sufficient consideration.

> *Glasbrook Bros v Glamorgan CC 1925*
> *The facts*: at a time of industrial unrest, colliery owners, rejecting the view of the police that a mobile force was enough, asked and agreed to pay for a special guard on the mine. Later they repudiated liability saying that the police had done no more than perform their public duty of maintaining order.

Decision: the extra services given, beyond what the police in their discretion deemed necessary, were consideration for the promise to pay. If the judgement of the police authorities had been that a special guard was necessary, they would not have been entitled to charge for it.

Where one party's actions lead to the need for heightened police presence, and the police deem this presence necessary, they may also be entitled to payment.

Harris v Sheffield United F.C. Ltd 1988
The facts: the defendants argued that they did not have to pay for a large police presence at their home matches.

Decision: they had voluntarily decided to hold matches on Saturday afternoons when large attendances were likely, increasing the risk of disorder. (An important factor here was that the police were required to be inside the football club's premises.)

Performance of more than existing contractual duties

If there is already a contract between A and B, and B promises additional reward to A if he (A) will perform his **existing duties**, there is **no consideration** from A to make that promise binding. A assumes no extra obligation and B obtains no extra rights or benefits.

Stilk v Myrick 1809
The facts: two members of the crew of a ship deserted in a foreign port. The master was unable to recruit substitutes and promised the rest of the crew that they should share the wages of the deserters if they would complete the voyage home short-handed. The shipowners however repudiated the promise.

Decision: in performing their existing contractual duties the crew gave no consideration for the promise of extra pay and the promise was not binding. The lack of two crew members did not mean that the remaining crew were doing more than their existing duty.

If a claimant does **more** than perform an existing contractual duty, this **may amount to consideration.**

Hartley v Ponsonby 1857
The facts: 17 men out of a crew of 36 deserted. The remainder were promised an extra £40 each to work the ship to Bombay. The claimant, one of the remaining crew-members, sued to recover this amount.

Decision: the large number of desertions made the voyage more hazardous, and this had the effect of discharging the original contract. The claimant had a new contract, under which his promise to complete the voyage formed consideration for the promise to pay an additional £40.

Recent developments

The courts appear to be taking a slightly different line in recent years on the payment of additional consideration.

Williams v Roffey Bros & Nicholls (Contractors) Ltd 1990

The facts: the claimants agreed to do carpentry work for the defendants, who were engaged as contractors to refurbish a block of flats, at a fixed price of £20,000. The work ran late and so the defendants, concerned that the job might not be finished on time and that they would have to pay under a penalty clause in the main contract, agreed to pay the claimants an extra £10,300 to ensure the work was completed on time. They later refused to pay the extra amount.

Decision: the fact that there was no apparent consideration for the promise to pay the extra was not held to be important, and in the court's view both parties derived benefit from the promise. The telling point was that the defendants' promise to pay the extra mount had not been extracted by duress or fraud: it was therefore binding.

Re Selectmove 1994

The facts: a company which was the subject of a winding-up order offered to settle its outstanding debts by instalment. An Inland Revenue inspector agreed to this proposal. The company tried to enforce it.

Decision: despite the verdict in *Williams v Roffey Bros & Nicholls*, the court followed *Foakes v Beer* (see below) in holding that an agreement to pay in instalments is unenforceable.

Performance of existing contractual duty to a third party

If A promises B a reward if B will perform his existing contract with C, there is consideration for A's promise since he has obtained a benefit to which he previously had no right, and B assumes new obligations.

Shadwell v Shadwell 1860

The facts: the claimant, a barrister, was engaged to marry E (an engagement to marry was at this time a binding contract). His uncle promised the claimant that if he married E (as he did), the uncle would during their joint lives pay £150 pa until such time as the nephew was earning 600 guineas (£630) working as a barrister (which never transpired). The uncle died after eighteen years, owing six annual payments. The claimant claimed the arrears from his uncle's executors, who denied that there was consideration for the promise.

Decision: the nephew had provided consideration as he was initially under a duty only to his fiancée, but by entering into the agreement he had put himself under obligation to the uncle too.

3 WAIVER OF EXISTING RIGHTS

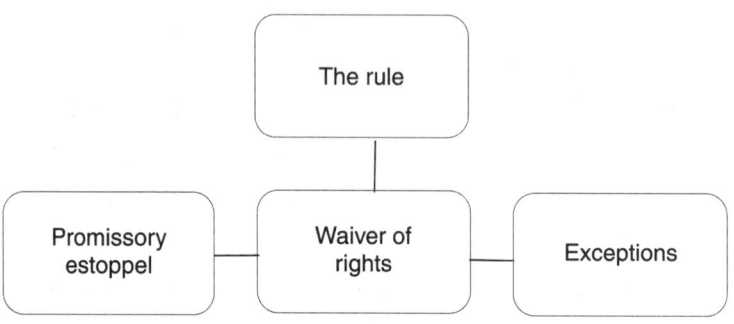

Particular complications arise over sufficiency of consideration for promises to **waive existing rights**, especially regarding rights to common law debts.

3.1 The rule

If X owes Y £100 but Y agrees to accept a lesser sum, say £80, in full settlement of Y's claim, that is a promise by Y to waive his entitlement to the balance of £20. The promise, like any other, should be supported by consideration. If it is not, it is not binding.

> *Foakes v Beer 1884*
> *The facts*: the defendant had obtained a court judgement against the claimant for the sum of £2,091. Judgement debts bear interest from the date of the judgement. By a written agreement the defendant agreed to accept payment by instalments of the sum of £2,091, no mention being made of the interest. Once the claimant had paid the amount of the debt in full, the defendant claimed interest, claiming that the agreement was not supported by consideration.
>
> *Decision*: she was entitled to the debt with interest. No consideration had been given by the claimant for waiver of any part of her rights against him.

3.2 Exceptions to the rule

There are, however, exceptions to the rule that the debtor (denoted by 'X' in the following paragraphs) must give consideration if the waiver is to be binding. These exceptions concern variation of the original contract terms.

(a) If X offers and Y accepts anything to which Y is not already entitled, the extra thing will be sufficient consideration for the waiver. This may be for example

   (i) Goods instead of cash: *Anon 1495* or
   (ii) Payment before the date payment is due: *Pinnel's case 1602.*

(b) If X arranges with a number of creditors that they will each accept part payment in full settlement, that is a bargain between the creditors. X has given no consideration but he can hold the creditors individually to the agreed terms: *Wood v Robarts 1818.*

(c) If a third party (Z) offers part payment and Y agrees to release X from Y's claim to the balance, Y has received consideration from Z against whom he had no previous claim.

Welby v Drake 1825
The facts: D owed W £18. D's father paid W £9 in settlement of the debt, and W had agreed to accept that amount. W then sued D for the remaining £9.

Decision: W could not recover the additional money, because the father, as a third party, had paid the original sum on the faith of the discharge of the sum from a further liability.

(d) The principle of **promissory estoppel** (see below) may prevent Y from retracting his promise with retrospective effect.

Activity 3 **(5 mins)**

Hugo agreed to drive his friend Laurence (a nervous passenger) to Cardiff. He said that if Laurence paid him £25, he would not exceed the speed limit on the motorway. Is this promise enforceable?

3.3 Promissory estoppel

The equitable concept of **promissory estoppel** operates to prevent a person rescinding (ie going back on) his promise to accept a lesser amount. He cannot retract his waiver with retrospective effect, though it may permit him to insist on full rights in the future.

Central London Property Trust v High Trees House 1947
The facts: in September 1939, the claimants let a block of flats to the defendants at an annual rent of £2,500 p.a. It was difficult to let the individual flats in wartime, so in January 1940, the claimants agreed in writing to accept a reduced rent of £1,250 p.a. No time limit was set on the arrangement but it was clearly related to wartime conditions. The reduced rent was paid from 1940 to 1945 and the defendants sublet flats during the period on the basis of their expected liability to pay rent under the head lease at £1,250 only. In 1945 the flats were fully let. The claimants demanded a full rent of £2,500 p.a., both retrospectively and for the future. They tested this claim by suing for rent at the full rate for the last two quarters of 1945.

Decision: the agreement of January 1940 was a temporary expedient only and had ceased to operate early in 1945. The claim was upheld. However, had the claimants sued for arrears for the period 1940-1945, the 1940 agreement would have served to defeat the claim.

Definition

> **Estoppel** operates when a person, by his words or conduct, leads another to believe that a certain state of affairs exists. If the other person, relying on that belief, alters his position to his detriment, the first person is **estopped** (prevented) from claiming later that a different state of affairs existed.

In the *High Trees* case, if the defendants had sued on the promise, they would have failed for want of consideration. The principle is '**a shield not a sword**', ie it is a defence, which does not create new rights.

> *Combe v Combe 1951*
> *The facts*: a wife obtained a divorce. Her ex-husband promised that he would make maintenance payments of £100 per annum. The wife did not apply to the court for an order for maintenance, but this forbearance was not at the husband's request. No maintenance was paid and the wife sued on the promise. In the High Court the wife obtained judgement on the basis of the principle of promissory estoppel. The ex-husband appealed.
>
> *Decision*: The Court of Appeal said that promissory estoppel 'does not create new causes of action where none existed before. It only prevents a party from insisting on his strict legal rights when it would be unjust to allow him to enforce them'. The wife's claim failed.

From this it can be seen that promissory estoppel applies only to a voluntary waiver of existing rights.

> *D and C Builders v Rees 1966*
> *The facts*: the defendants owed £482 to the claimants. The claimants, who were in acute financial difficulties, reluctantly agreed to accept £300 in full settlement. They later claimed the balance.
>
> *Decision*: the debt must be paid in full. Promissory estoppel only applies to a promise voluntarily given. The defendants had been aware of and had exploited the claimants' difficulties. In this important case it was also held that payment by cheque (instead of in cash) is normal and gives no extra advantage which could be treated as consideration for the waiver under the rule in *Pinnel's case*.

Summary

Promissory estoppel is one of the most complex legal doctrines you will encounter in this book. In summary, three elements are required if promissory estoppel is to apply:

- A waiver of rights by one of the parties to the contract
- The other party must rely on that waiver to some extent
- Some special or unusual circumstances must apply

These three components can be clearly illustrated by the *High Trees* case, as follows.

- Central London Property trust waived their right to the full rent while subletting was difficult

- High Trees relied on that waiver by in turn reducing the rents charged to their tenants

- The situation arose because of the war: an unusual set of circumstances

4 PRIVITY OF CONTRACT

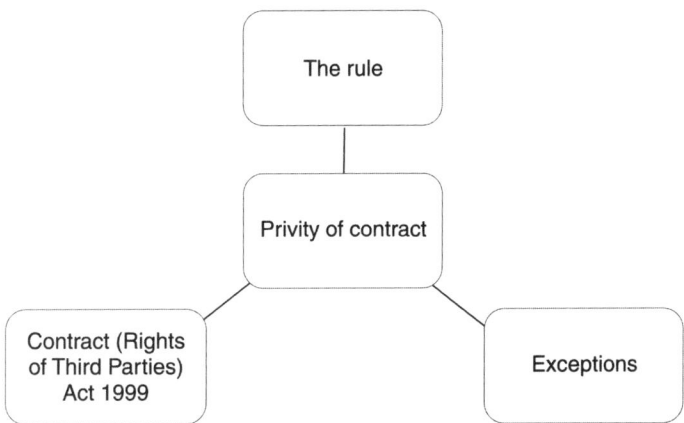

If you don't provide consideration, you cannot sue on the contract. This is a critical rule in contract law, and reflects the fact that consideration is essential.

This maxim means that **only the person who has paid the price of a contract can sue on it.** If, for example, A promises B that (for a consideration provided by B) A will confer a benefit on C, then C cannot as a general rule enforce A's promise.

> *Tweddle v Atkinson 1861*
> *The facts*: the claimant married the daughter of G. On the occasion of the marriage, the claimant's father and G exchanged promises that they would each pay a sum of money to the claimant. The agreement between the two fathers expressly provided that the claimant should have enforceable rights against them. G died without making the promised payment and the claimant sued G's executor for the specified amount.
>
> *Decision*: the claimant had provided no consideration for G's promise. In spite of the express terms of the agreement he had no enforceable rights under it and was not therefore 'privy to the contract'.

In *Tweddle's* case each father as promisee gave consideration by his promise to the other, but the claimant was to be the beneficiary of each promise. Each father could have sued the other but the claimant could not sue.

The rule that consideration must move from the promisee overlaps with the rule that only a party to a contract can enforce it. Together these rules are known as the principles of **privity of contract**.

No-one may be entitled to or bound by the terms of a contract to which he is not an original party. A person is regarded as a party to the contract if he provides consideration.

4.1 The rule

As a general rule, only a person who is a party to a contract has enforceable rights or obligations under it. The following is the leading case in this area:

> *Dunlop v Selfridge 1915*
>
> *The facts*: the claimant, a tyre manufacturer, supplied tyres to X, a distributor, on terms that X would not re-sell the tyres at less than the prescribed retail price. If X sold the tyres wholesale to trade customers, X must impose a similar condition on those buyers to observe minimum retail prices (such clauses were legal at the time though prohibited since 1964 by the Resale Prices Act). X resold tyres on these conditions to the defendant. Under the terms of the contract between X and Selfridge, Selfridge was to pay to the claimant a sum of £5 per tyre if it sold tyres to customers below the minimum retail price. They sold tyres to two customers at less than the minimum price. The claimant sued to recover £5 per tyre as liquidated damages.
>
> *Decision*: the claimant could not recover damages under a contract (between X and Selfridge) to which it was not a party.

Definition

> **Privity of contract** is the relation between the two parties to a contract. Third parties who are not privy to the contract generally have no right of action. This is true even if they receive benefits under it.

Effect on third parties

In these circumstances the party to the contract who imposes the condition or obtains a promise of a benefit for a third party can usually enforce it, but damages cannot be recovered on the third party's behalf unless the contracting party is suing an agent or trustee. Only nominal damages can be given if the contract was only for a third party's benefit. Other remedies may be sought however.

> *Beswick v Beswick 1968*
>
> *The facts*: X transferred his business to the defendant, his nephew, in consideration for a pension of £6.50 per week and, after his death, a weekly annuity to X's widow. Only one such annuity payment was made. The widow brought an action against the nephew, asking for an order of specific performance. She sued both as administratrix of her husband's estate and in her personal capacity as recipient.
>
> *Decision*: as her husband's representative, the widow was successful in enforcing the contract for a third party's (her own) benefit. In her personal capacity she could derive no right of action.

Exception to the third party rule

Where the contract is one which provides something for the enjoyment of both the contracting party and third parties, such as a family holiday, the contracting party may be entitled to recover damages for his loss of the benefit.

Jackson v Horizon Holidays Ltd 1975
The facts: Mr Jackson booked a holiday with Horizon for himself and his family. Various things went wrong and the holiday did not meet the claims of the brochure, and Mr Jackson sued for damages for his own loss and disappointment and that of his family.

Decision: He was successful in claiming all of the damages as the contract was made not only for Mr Jackson himself but also for the benefit and enjoyment of his family. This judgement has been fairly widely criticised.

FOR DISCUSSION

Do you think that the judgement in *Jackson, v Horizon Holidays* was fair, or do you think it breached legal principles? What source of law (from Chapter 2) do you think is demonstrated here?

If the contract is broken and the claimant seeks damages on the other parties' behalf he can also recover for the loss suffered by those other people: Woodar Investment Development Ltd v Wimpey Construction (UK) Ltd 1980.

4.2 Exceptions

There are a number of real or apparent exceptions to the general rule of privity of contract.

(a) *Implied trusts*

   Equity may hold that an implied trust has been created.

   Gregory and Parker v Williams 1817
   The facts: P owed money to G and W. He agreed with W to transfer his property to W if W would pay his (P's) debt to G. The property was transferred, but W refused to pay G. G could not sue on the contract between P and W.

   Decision: P could be regarded as a trustee for G, and G would therefore bring an action jointly with P.

(b) *Statutory exceptions*

   (i) There are statutory exceptions which permit a person injured in a road accident to claim against the **motorist's insurers** (Road Traffic Act 1972) and which permit husband or wife to **insure his or her own life** for the benefit of the other under a trust which the beneficiary can enforce (Married Woman's Property Act 1882).

   (ii) The provisions of the Contract (Rights of Third Parties) Act 1999 has had a significant impact on the rights of third parties, see below.

(c) *Agency*

   (i) In normal circumstances the **agent** discloses to a third party with whom he contracts that he is acting for a principal whose identity is also disclosed. The agent has no liability under the contract and no right to enforce it.

(ii) If a person enters into a contract apparently on his own account but in fact as agent on behalf of a principal, the doctrine of the **undisclosed principal** determines the position of the parties. An undisclosed principal may adopt a contract made for him by an agent. Until such time as the principal takes this action, the agent himself may sue the third party.

(d) *Covenants*

A restrictive covenant, which a third party may enforce, may run with land. For example, if the owner of a house is bound by a covenant not to cut down trees on the land, any subsequent buyer of that house will also be bound by the same covenant.

(e) *Assignment*

(i) A party to a contract can **assign** or transfer to another person **the rights** contained in the contract. He cannot assign the burden of his contractual **obligations**.

(ii) A legal assignment must be absolute, it must be in writing, and notice must be given to the other party: s 136 Law of Property Act 1925. It is **not possible** to assign:

(1) A **right of action**, which is a claim for unliquidated damages for breach of contract

(2) **Rights which are personal** to the original parties to the contract.

Activity 4 (10 mins)

Julia arranges a party for her daughter Tamsin's 21st birthday, and books the band 'Mardi Gras'. On the day, the band fail to turn up and Tamsin is distraught. Who can sue them for breach of contract?

4.3 Contracts (Rights of Third Parties) Act 1999

The Contracts (Rights of Third Parties) Act 1999 gives third parties statutory rights under contracts in certain circumstances.

There is a two-limbed test for the circumstances in which a third party may enforce a contract term:

- Whether the contract itself expressly so provides

- Where the term confers a benefit on the third party, unless it appears that the contracting parties did not intend him to have the right to enforce it.

The third party must be expressly identified in the contract by name, class or description, but need not be in existence when the contract is made (for example, an unborn child or future spouse).

Chapter roundup

- 'A valuable consideration in the sense of the law may consist either in some right, interest, profit or benefit accruing to one party, or some forbearance, detriment, loss or responsibility given, suffered or undertaken by the other.' *Currie v Misa 1875.*

- Consideration may be executed (an act in return for a promise) or executory (a promise in return for a promise). It may not be past, unless one of three recognised exceptions applies.

- Consideration need not be adequate, but it must be sufficient. This means that what is tendered as consideration must be capable in law of being regarded as consideration, but need not necessarily be equal in value to the consideration received in return (for example a peppercorn rent).

- The principle of promissory estoppel was developed in *Central London Property Trust v High Trees House 1947.*

- As a general rule, only a person who is a party to a contract has enforceable rights or obligations under it. This is the doctrine of privity of contract, as demonstrated in *Dunlop v Selfridge 1915.*

Quick quiz

1 What is executed consideration?

2 What is past consideration?

3 Give three situations where past consideration may make a promise binding.

4 What point of law is illustrated by *Chappell & Co v Nestle Co 1960?*

5 Summarise the facts of *Stilk v Myrick 1809* and *Hartley v Ponsonby 1857*, showing the distinction between them.

6 List two situations in which a debtor need not give consideration for a creditor who promises to accept a lesser sum in full settlement of a debt to be bound by his promise.

7 What is the doctrine of promissory estoppel?

8 What is privity of contract?

9 Give the name of a case which illustrates the rule that consideration must move from the promisee.

Answers to quick quiz

1 An act which has been performed (executed) in return for a promise.

2 Anything which has been done before a promise is made to do something in return.

3 Bills of exchange
Elapse of time
Request for services

4 Consideration need not be adequate.

5   In Stilk v Myrick, 2 of the crew deserted, and the fact that the rest of the crew sailed the ship home was not sufficient consideration. In Hartley v Ponsonby, half of the crew deserted. The sailing home of the ship by the remainder **was** sufficient consideration for the wages promised.

6   Part payment by a third party.

   The offer of something different, eg goods instead of cash.

7   It prevents someone going back on a promise to accept less consideration in certain circumstances.

8   The rule that only the parties to a contract (ie those who provide consideration) may sue on it.

9   *Tweddle v Atkinson, 1861*

Answers to activities

1   (b) and (c). (a) is not as consideration is past. (b) is executory consideration and (c) gives rise to an implied promise to pay, as in *Lampleigh v Braithwait 1615.*

2   (b) only. Consideration need only be sufficient, it need not be adequate (a). It can be past in limited circumstances (c). It need not be given in a contract by deed (d). Performance of an existing obligation cannot support a new contract (e) because there is no extra obligation.

3   No, as by keeping within the speed limit, Hugo is doing no more than his existing legal duty. He is not doing anything 'extra'.

4   Only Julia, as she was privy to the contract, while Tamsin is not.

Assignment 2   (45 mins)

In 20X8, Ann, an artist, decided to have an extension built onto her house. She agreed to pay Belle £500 to produce the architectural plans for the work and Chas £3,000 for carrying out the work. Ann provided all the materials, which she bought from Dan for an agreed price of £5,000. After the work was completed Ann discovered that she did not actually have the money to pay the various people concerned. Consequently she made the following arrangements with each of them:

(a) She gave Belle one of her paintings instead of payment.

(b) When she failed to pay Chas he threatened to sue her, until her friend Eric offered to pay him £1,500 if he withdrew his action, which he did.

(c) She told Dan that he would have accept £3,000 as she could not afford to pay him any more money and he reluctantly agreed to accept it in full and final payment of her debt.

Three months later Ann inherited £100,000.

Task

Advise the parties whether Ann can be made to pay her original debts.

Chapter 6 :

INTENTION, CAPACITY AND FORM

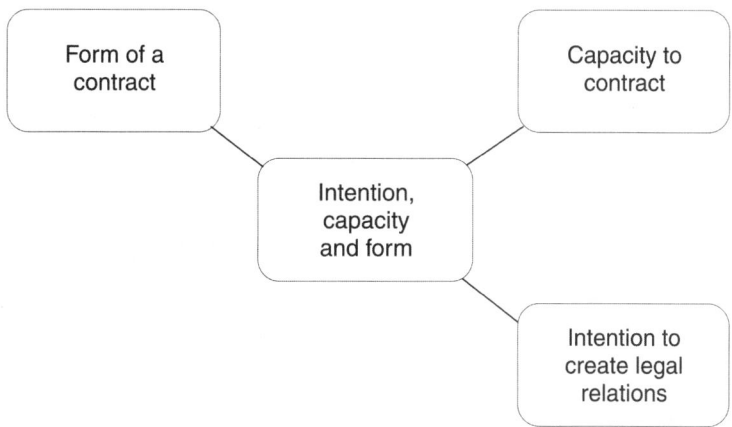

Introduction

An agreement is not a binding contract unless the parties intend to create legal relations and have the capacity or ability to do so. 'Legal relations' can be defined as the willingness to be bound by the terms of the contract. Where there is no express statement as to whether or not legal relations are intended (as may be said to be true of the majority of contracts), the courts apply one of two presumptions:

(a) Social, domestic and family arrangements are *not* usually intended by the parties involved to be binding;

(b) Commercial agreements *are* usually intended to be legally binding.

Anyone entering a contract has to have the capacity to do so, otherwise it can be argued that they are not acting in full understanding of what they are doing. The law seeks to protect such groups of people, most notably those aged under 18, known as minors.

Most contracts can be in any form, but there are rules to govern certain specific types of contract.

Your objectives

In this chapter you will learn about the following.

(a) The rules governing when spouses enter a contract with each other

(b) The rules governing commercial agreements

(c) The rules governing capacity to contract

(d) The rules governing the form of a contract

1 INTENTION TO CREATE LEGAL RELATIONS

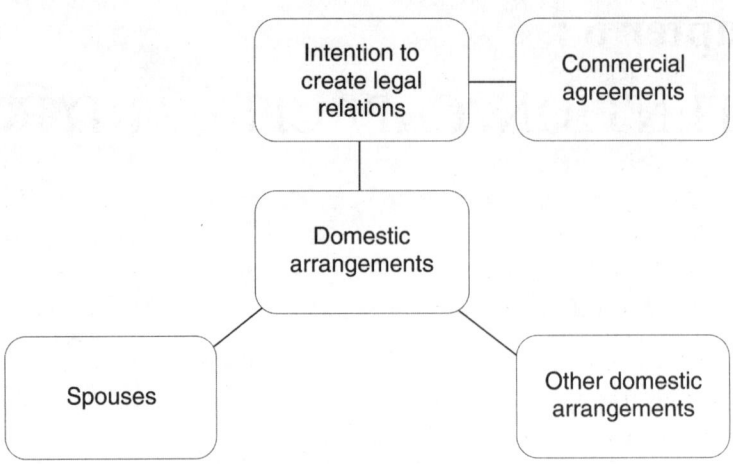

1.1 Domestic arrangements

In most agreements no intention is expressly stated. If it is a domestic agreement between husband and wife, relatives or friends it is presumed that there is no intention to create legal relations unless the circumstances point to the opposite conclusion.

1.2 Spouses

However, where agreements between husband and wife or other relatives relate to property matters, the courts may well impute an intention to create legal relations.

> *Balfour v Balfour 1919*
> The husband was employed in Ceylon. He and his wife returned to the UK on leave but it was agreed that for health reasons she would not return to Ceylon with him. He promised to pay her £30 a month as maintenance. Later the marriage ended in divorce and the wife sued for the monthly allowance which the husband no longer paid.
>
> *Held*: an informal agreement of indefinite duration made between husband and wife (whose marriage had not then broken up) was not intended to be legally binding.

Contrast this with:

> *Merritt v Merritt 1970*
> The husband had left the matrimonial home, which was owned in the joint name of husband and wife, to live with another woman. The spouses met and held a discussion in the husband's car in the course of which he agreed to pay her £40 a month out of which she agreed to keep up the mortgage payments on the house. The wife refused to leave the car until the husband signed a note of these agreed terms and an undertaking to transfer the house into her sole name when the mortgage had been paid off. The wife paid off the mortgage but the husband refused to transfer the house to her.
>
> *Held*: in the circumstances, an intention to create legal relations was to be inferred and the wife could sue for breach of contract.

1.3 Other domestic arrangements

Domestic arrangements extend to those between people who are not related but who have a close relationship of some form. The nature of the agreement itself may lead to the conclusion that legal relations were intended.

> *Simpkins v Pays 1955*
> The defendant, her granddaughter and the claimant, a paying boarder, took part together in a weekly competition organised by a Sunday newspaper. The arrangements were informal and the entries were made in the grandmother's name. One week they won £750 but the paying boarder was denied a third share by the other two.
>
> *Held*: there was a 'mutuality in the arrangements between the parties', amounting to a joint enterprise. As such it was not a 'friendly adventure' as the defendant claimed, but a contract.

1.4 Commercial agreements

When businessmen enter into commercial agreements it is presumed that there is an intention to enter into legal relations unless this is expressly disclaimed or the circumstances displace that presumption. Any express statement by the parties of their intention not to make a binding contract is conclusive.

> *Rose and Frank v JR Compton & Bros 1923*
> A commercial agreement by which the defendants (a British manufacturer) appointed the claimants to be their distributor in the USA expressly stated that it was 'not subject to legal jurisdiction' in either country. The defendants terminated the agreement without giving notice as required, and refused to deliver goods ordered by the claimants, although they had accepted these orders when placed.
>
> *Held*: the general agreement was not legally binding, but the orders for goods were separate and binding contracts. The claim for damages for breach of the agreement failed, but the claim for damages for non-delivery of goods ordered succeeded.

> *Edwards v Skyways Ltd 1964*
> In negotiations over the terms for making an employee redundant, the employer undertook to make an ex gratia (effectively a voluntary) payment to him.
>
> *Held*: although the defendants argued that the use of the phrase ex gratia showed no intention to create legal relations, this was a commercial arrangement and the burden of refuting the presumption of legal relations had not been discharged by them.

Procedural agreements between employers and trade unions for the settlement of disputes are not by their nature intended to give rise to legal relations in spite of their elaborate and very legal contents: s 179 Trade Union and Labour Relations (Consolidation) Act 1992.

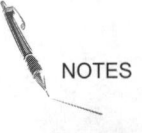

NOTES

Activity 1 (5 mins)

A widow tells her adult son that he can stay at her house temporarily so long as he does his share of domestic chores. Consider whether there is likely to be a contract under which accommodation is supplied in return for housework. Give reasons for your answer.

Activity 2 (10 mins)

Which of the following scenarios do you think gives rise to the intention to create legal relations?

(a) Jenny, a student, offers to pay her brother Jim if he will help her with an assignment. Jim has helped but Jenny will not pay up.

(b) Mary and her friend Bridget regularly play bingo together. When they started doing so, they both signed a piece of paper to the effect that if either of them ever won more than £100, the money would be shared equally. Mary has now won £70,000 and is refusing to pay any proportion of it to Bridget.

(c) Dave, a taxi driver, agrees to take Brian to the airport. Brian will pay the full fare. Dave now says that he would rather go to watch a football match and will not therefore be taking Brian.

2 CAPACITY TO CONTRACT

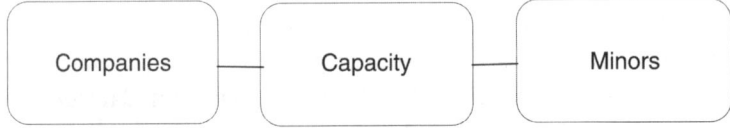

Capacity refers to the fact that the law regards some groups as being unable to enter into binding contractual arrangements, because they might not be in a position to fully understand the agreement they have entered into.

3.1 Minors

The legal capacity of minors (persons under the age of 18) is determined by the Minors' Contracts Act 1987. A contract between a minor and another party may be one of three types.

- A **valid** contract is binding in the usual way.

- A **voidable** contract is binding unless and until the minor rescinds the contract.

- An **unenforceable** contract is unenforceable against the minor unless he ratifies (adopts) it - but the other party is bound.

Two sorts of contract are valid and binding on a minor: a contract for the supply of goods or services which are **necessaries,** and a **service contract** for the minor's benefit.

If goods or services which are necessaries are delivered to a minor under a contract made by him, he is bound to pay a reasonable price for them: s 3 Sale of Goods Act 1979. Necessaries are defined in s 3 Sale of Goods Act 1979 as goods or services **suitable** to the condition in life of the minor and to his **needs** at the time of sale and delivery.

(a)   **Suitability** is measured by the living standards of the minor. Things may be necessaries even though they are luxurious in quality, if that is what the minor ordinarily uses. Food, clothing, professional advice and even a gold watch have been held to be necessaries.

(b)   The second test is whether the minor requires the goods for the personal **needs** of himself (or his wife or child). Goods required for use in a trade are not necessaries, nor are goods of any kind if the minor is already well supplied with them.

Nash v Inman 1908
The facts: N was a London tailor who sued I on bills totalling £145 for clothes, including eleven fancy waistcoats. It was conceded that the clothes were suitable, but it was shown that he already had plenty of them.
Decision: the clothes were not necessaries.

A **service contract** for the minor's benefit which contains an element of education or training is the other type of contract which is binding on a minor.

Doyle v White City Stadium 1935
The facts: D, who was a minor, obtained a licence to compete as a professional boxer. Under his licence (which was treated as a contract of apprenticeship) he agreed to be bound by rules which could withhold his prize money if he was disqualified for a foul blow (as in fact happened). He asserted that the licence was a void contract since it was not for his benefit..

Decision: the licence enabled him to pursue a lucrative occupation. Despite the penal clause, it was beneficial as a whole.

Voidable contracts of a minor

A minor may enter into a contract by which he acquires an interest of a continuing nature. Such contracts are **voidable** by the minor during his minority and within a reasonable time after attaining his majority. If no such steps are taken, the contract is binding. Examples of voidable contracts are:

*   Contracts concerning **land** - for example, leases.
*   Purchases of **shares** in a company.
*   **Partnership** agreements.

A contract of this type does not require any kind of ratification by the minor on his majority. It remains binding unless he **repudiates** it within a reasonable time.

Edwards v Carter 1893
The facts: A marriage settlement was made under which the father of the husband to be agreed to pay £1,500 per annum to the trustees. The husband to be, who was a minor at the time of the settlement, executed a deed under which all property which he might receive under his father's will would also be vested in the trustees. He attained his majority one month later, and three

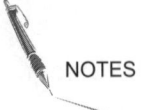
and a half years later his father died. A year after this, he repudiated the agreement.

Decision: the repudiation was too late and was ineffective.

The effect of repudiation is to relieve the minor of any contractual obligations arising after the repudiation. The key to liability or recovery of sums paid may well depend upon whether the minor received **consideration**.

> *Steinberg v Scala (Leeds) 1923*
> *The facts:* The claimant bought shares in the defendant company but repudiated the contract after paying some of the money. The company agreed to remove her name from the register of members but refused to refund her money.
>
> *Decision:* the claimant had benefited from membership rights as consideration, and was not entitled to a refund.

Unenforceable contracts of a minor

All other contracts entered into by a minor are described as **unenforceable** - the minor is not bound (though he may ratify it) but the other party is bound.

Where a contract is voidable and is repudiated by the minor, or where it is unenforceable and is not ratified by the minor, any **guarantee** of the contract given by a capable (ie adult) person is still valid. In addition, a minor may be required to return property which he acquired under a repudiated or unenforceable contract.

A minor is generally liable for his **torts** (ie wrongful acts causing loss or damage to others). He will not, however, be liable if he commits a tort in procuring a contract which is not binding on him. If he were liable, the other party would effectively be able to enforce such a contract.

> *R Leslie Ltd v Sheill 1914*
> *The facts*: An infant obtained a loan of £400 by means of a fraudulent misstatement of his age.
>
> *Decision:* he could not be compelled to repay it, as this would constitute enforcement of the contract.

FOR DISCUSSION

The law relating to minors' contracts has remained unchanged for decades. Do you think that it should be changed? Would you retain the same amount of protection for minors?

2.2 Companies

The capacity of a company to contract may be restricted by one of its 'constitution documents', the memorandum of association. An act by the company which exceeds its capacity is said to be *ultra vires*.

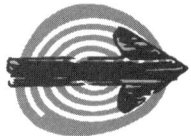

The purpose of this is to protect the shareholders of a company and its creditors, to prevent the directors from causing the company to enter contracts that might be to the detriment of the interests of the shareholders and creditors.

Company law, including the capacity of companies to contract, is covered in Specialist Unit 44.

3 FORM OF A CONTRACT

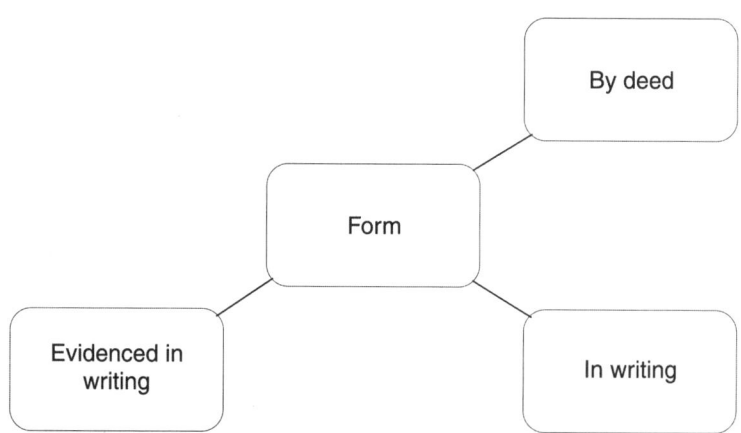

One of the most widely held misapprehensions about contracts is that they have to be in writing and signed by both parties.

For example, a customer in a self-service shop may take his selected goods to the cash desk, pay for them and walk out without saying a word. The three essential elements of a contract (offer, acceptance, consideration and the intention to create legal relations) are present and a contract of sale has been formed.

Writing makes it easier to prove the contents of the contract, but it is not usually necessary unless related to one of the following:

- Some contracts must be by **deed**
- Some contracts must be in **writing**
- Some contracts must be **evidenced in writing**

3.1 Contracts by deed

Under s 1 Law of Property (Miscellaneous Provisions) Act 1989, contracts relating to the transfer of land must be by deed, **in writing, signed and witnessed**. Delivery is conduct indicating that the parties intend to be bound by the contract.

Contracts which must be by deed include the following.

- **Leases** for three years or more

- A **conveyance** or transfer of a legal estate in land (including a mortgage). This is the 'completion' on the sale of a house.

- A **promise not supported by consideration** (such as a covenant to make annual payments to a charity)

Contracts made by deed are also referred to as specialty contracts.

3.2 Contracts which must be in writing

Some types of contract are required to be in the form of a written document, usually signed by at least one of the parties. Contracts which must be in writing include the following.

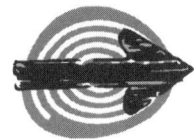

- A **transfer of shares** in a limited company
- The **sale** or **disposition of an interest in land** (the 'exchange of contracts' on the sale of a house)
- **Bills of exchange** and **cheques**
- **Consumer credit** contracts

In the case of consumer credit transactions, the effect of non-compliance by the seller (failure to make a regulated consumer credit agreement in the prescribed form) is to make the agreement unenforceable against the debtor unless the creditor obtains a court order. This is covered in more depth in Unit 26, Business Law.

3.3 Contracts which must be evidenced in writing

Certain contracts may be made orally, but are not enforceable in a court of law unless there is written evidence of their terms. The most important contract of this type is the contract of guarantee. A signed note of the material terms of the contract is sufficient.

FOR DISCUSSION

In modern time, many contracts are now formed electronically, with increased use of 'e-commerce'. What legal issues might electronic contracts raise?

Chapter roundup

- An agreement is not binding unless the parties intend to be bound by it.
- Legal relations are not normally intended in domestic situations (although there are exceptions to this).
- Legal relations are presumed to be intended in commercial agreements, unless clearly indicated otherwise.
- Some legal persons may have restricted capacity to contract, for example minors and companies.
- Generally a contract may be made in any form, although there are some exceptions to this rule.

Quick quiz

1   Contrast *Balfour v Balfour* with *Merritt v Merritt* and explain why they had different outcomes

2   What general rule applies in commercial agreements?

3   What contracts made by minors are valid?

4   What contracts must be evidenced in writing?

Answers to quick quiz

1   In Balfour v Balfour, the couple were still married at the time of the agreement, so it was not legally binding. In Merritt v Merritt, the couple were legally separating, so the agreement was legally binding.

2   They are presumed to be legally binding.

3   Contracts for the supply of goods and services which are necessaries.

    Service contracts for the minor's benefit.

4   A contract of guarantee

Answers to activities

1   No there is unlikely to be a contract, as in this domestic situation legal relations are unlikely to be intended.

2   (a)   The parties to a social or domestic arrangement are presumed not to have intended to create legal relations. A brother and sister would be regarded as being within a 'domestic' situation. Therefore Jim will not be able to enforce the agreement.

    (b)   On the face of it, this would appear to be a domestic arrangement, as it involves two friends socialising together. Therefore there would not be an intention to create legal relations. However, given that Mary and Bridget both signed a piece of paper stating what should happen, it can be argued that legal relations were intended. Bridget should be able to claim half of Mary's winnings.

    (c)   This would appear to be a commercial agreement and the intention to create legal relations is therefore presumed. Brian should be able to act against Dave for breach of contract.

Assignment 3   **(30 minutes)**

Explain whether the intention to create legal relations is an essential element in a binding contract.

Guidance notes

1   Social, domestic and family arrangements are assumed not to be legally binding unless the contrary is clearly shown.

2   Commercial agreements are assumed to be legally binding unless the contrary is clearly shown.

PART B

SPECIFIC TERMS IN A BUSINESS CONTRACT

Chapter 7 :
TERMS AND EXCLUSION CLAUSES

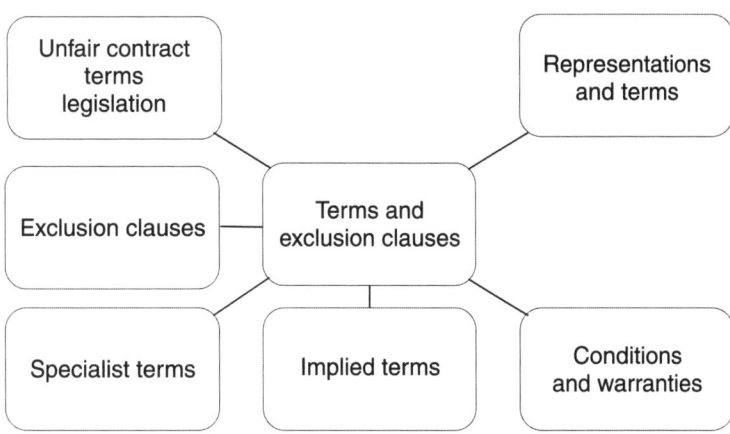

Introduction

As a general principle the parties may by their offer and acceptance include in their contract whatever terms they like, but certain legal rules apply and the law may modify these express terms in various ways.

(a) The terms must be sufficiently complete and precise to produce an agreement which can be binding. If they are vague there may be no contract.

(b) Statements made in the pre-contract negotiations may become *terms* of the contract or remain as *representations* to which different rules attach.

(c) The terms of the contract are usually classified as *conditions* or as *warranties* according to their importance.

(d) In addition to the express terms of the agreement, additional terms may be implied by law.

(e) Terms which exclude or restrict liability for breach of contract (exemption or exclusion clauses) are restricted in their effect or overridden by common law and statutory rules.

Your objectives

In this chapter you will learn about the following.

(a) The effects of incompleteness in the terms of a contract

(b) The distinction between representations and contract terms

(c) The concepts of condition, warranty and innominate term

(d) How terms may be implied into a contract

(e) Some examples of specialist terms in a contracts

(f)   The limitations on the effectiveness of exclusion clauses

(g)   How exclusion clauses may fail to be effectively incorporated into a contract

(h)   How exclusion clauses are interpreted

(i)   The main provisions of the Unfair Contract Terms Act 1977

1   REPRESENTATIONS AND TERMS

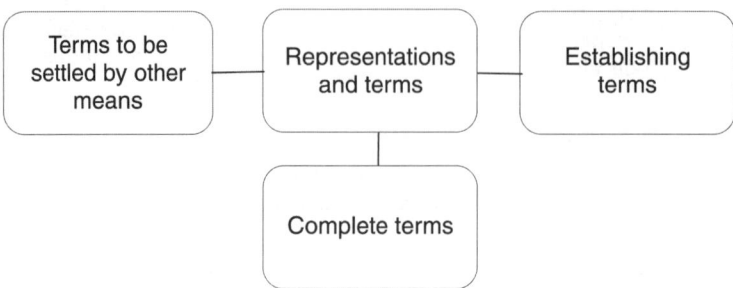

If something said in pre-contract negotiations proves to be untrue, the party misled can only claim for breach of contract if the statement became a term of the contract. Otherwise his remedy is for misrepresentation only, whereby the contract is voidable.

1.1   Establishing contract terms

Even if the statement is not repeated or referred to in making the contract it may be treated as a contract term. But such factors as a significant interval of time between statement and contract, or the use of a written contract making no reference to the statement suggest that it is not a term of the contract. If, however, the party who makes the statement speaks with special knowledge of the subject it is more likely to be treated as a contract term.

Bannerman v White 1861

In negotiations for the sale of hops the buyer emphasised that it was essential to him that the hops should not have been treated with sulphur. The seller replied explicitly that no sulphur had been used. It was later discovered that a small proportion of the hops (bought in by the seller from another grower) had been treated with sulphur. The buyer refused to pay the price.

Held: the representation as to the absence of sulphur was intended to be a term of the contract.

Oscar Chess v Williams 1959

A private motorist negotiated the sale of an old car to motor dealers in part exchange for a new car. The seller stated (as the registration book showed) that his car was a 1948 model and the dealer valued it at £280. In fact it was a 1939 model worth only £175 (the registration book had been altered by a previous owner).

Held: the statement was a mere representation. The seller was not an expert and the buyer had better means of discovering the truth.

1.2   Complete terms

A legally binding agreement must be complete in its term otherwise there is no contract since the parties are still at the stage of negotiating the necessary terms.

> *Scammell v Ouston 1941*
>
> An agreement for the purchase of a van provided that the unpaid balance of the price should be paid over two years 'on hire purchase terms'.
>
> *Held:* there was no agreement since it was uncertain what terms of payment were intended. Hire purchase terms vary as to intervals between payments, interest charges to be added, and so on.

1.3   Terms to be settled by other means

It is always possible for the parties to leave an essential term to be settled by specified means outside the contract. For example, it may be agreed to sell at the ruling open market price (if there is a market) on the day of delivery, or to invite an arbitrator to determine a fair price. The price may even be determined by the course of dealing between the parties: *Hillas & Co Ltd v Arcos Ltd 1932*.

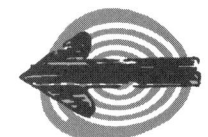

Hillas Ltd v Arcos Ltd was covered in Chapter 4, Section 1.1. Refer back to that for details.

If the parties use meaningless but non-essential words, for example by use of standard printed conditions some of which are inappropriate, such phrases may be disregarded.

> *Nicolene v Simmonds 1953*
> *The facts:* In the wording of a contract there was the phrase 'We are in agreement that the usual conditions of acceptance apply.' In fact there were no 'usual conditions of acceptance' so the words were meaningless, but one of the parties was trying to argue that the contract was unenforceable as it was not complete.
>
> *Decision:* the contract was enforceable as the clause was so meaningless that it could be ignored, and still leave the contract valid and understandable.

If however the parties expressly agree to defer some essential term for later negotiation there is no binding agreement. This is described as 'an agreement to agree' which is void, as the parties may subsequently fail to agree.

Activity 1   **(5 mins)**

A contract contains a term which states that the price shall be £50,000 unless the parties agree otherwise within seven days of the contract's being signed.

Does this invalidate the contract? Give reasons for your answer.

2 CONDITIONS AND WARRANTIES

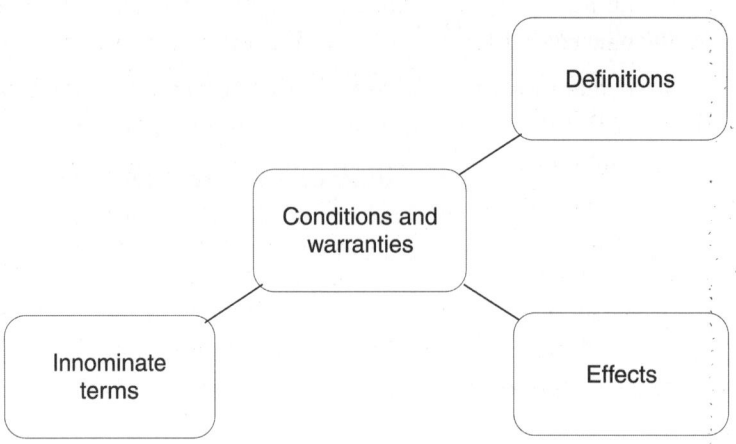

2.1 Definitions

The terms of the contract are usually classified by their relative importance as conditions or warranties.

Definitions

Condition: a term which is vital to the contract, going to the root of the contract.

Warranty: a less important term. It does not go to the root of the contract, but is subsidiary to the main purpose of the agreement.

2.2 Effects

Non-observance of a condition will affect the main purpose of the agreement. Breach of a condition entitles the party not in breach to treat the contract as discharged. Breach of a warranty only entitles the injured party to claim damages.

The following two cases are very useful in highlighting the difference.

> *Poussard v Spiers 1876*
> Madame Poussard agreed to sing in an opera throughout a series of performances. Owing to illness she was unable to appear on the opening night or on the next few days. The producer engaged a substitute who insisted that she should be engaged for the whole run. When Mme Poussard had recovered, the producer declined to accept her services for the remaining performances.
>
> *Held:* failure to sing on the opening night was a breach of condition which entitled the producer to treat the contract for the remaining performances as discharged. Singing on the opening night could be regarded as fundamental to the contract.

Contrast that with:

> *Bettini v Gye 1876*
>
> An opera singer was engaged for a series of performances under a contract by which he had to be in London for rehearsals six days before the opening performance. Owing to illness he did not arrive until the third day before the opening. The defendant refused to accept his services, treating the contract as discharged.
>
> *Held:* the rehearsal clause was subsidiary to the main purpose of the contract. The contract did not fail because the singer missed some of the rehearsals. Breach of the clause must be treated as breach of warranty, so the producer was bound to accept the singer's services. He had no right to treat the contract as discharged and must compensate the claimant, though he could claim damages (if he could prove any loss) for failure to arrive in time for six days' rehearsals.

Consider also:

> *Schuler v Wickham Machine Tool Sales 1973*
>
> The claimants entered into a four-year contract with the defendants giving them the sole right to sell panel presses in England. A clause of the contract provided that it should be a condition of the agreement that the defendants' representative should visit six named firms each week to solicit orders. The defendants' representative failed on a few occasions to do so and the claimants claimed to be entitled to repudiate the agreement on the basis that a single failure was a breach of condition giving them an absolute right to treat the contract as at an end.
>
> *Held:* such minor breaches by the defendants did not entitle the claimants to repudiate. The House of Lords construed the clause on the basis that it was so unreasonable that the parties could not have intended it as a condition (giving the claimants a right of repudiation) but rather as a warranty. Thus the claimants were themselves in breach of contract leaving the defendants with a claim for damages against them.

Determining whether a contractual term is a condition or a warranty is clearly very important. Classification depends on the following issues.

(a)   Statute often identifies implied terms specifically as conditions or warranties. Such identification must be followed by the courts. An example is the Sale of Goods Act 1979 which states, for example, that in a contract for the sale of goods there is an implied condition that the seller has the legal authority to sell.

(b)   Case law may also define particular clauses as conditions, for example a clause as to the date of 'expected readiness' of a ship let to a charterer: *The Mihalis Angelos 1971*.

(c)   Where statute or case law does not shed any light, the court will consider the intention of the parties **at the time the contract was made** as to whether a broken term was to be a condition or a warranty.

2.3   Innominate terms

Where the term broken was not clearly intended to be a condition, and neither statute nor case law define it as such, it cannot necessarily be assumed that the term is a

warranty. Instead, **the contract must be interpreted in the light of the specific situation**; only if it is clear that in no circumstances did the parties intend the contract to be terminated by breach of that particular term can it be classed as a warranty. Such intention may be **express** or be **implied** from surrounding circumstances. Where it is not clear what the effect of breach of the term was intended to be, it will be classified by the court as innominate, intermediate or indeterminate (the three are synonymous).

The consequence of a term being classified as innominate is that the court must decide what is the actual effect of its breach. So it does not fall neatly into the classification of either condition or warranty and therefore cannot follow the rules for those. If the nature and effect of the breach is such as to deprive the injured party of substantially the whole benefit which it was intended he should obtain under the contract, then it will be treated as a breached condition, so that the injured party may terminate the contract and claim damages.

> *Hong Kong Fir Shipping Co Ltd v Kawasaki Kisa Kaisha Ltd 1962*
> *The facts:* The defendants chartered a ship from the claimants for a period of 24 months. A term in the contract stated that the claimants would provide a ship which was 'in every way fitted for ordinary cargo service'. They were in breach of this term since the ship required a competent engine room crew which they did not provide. Because of the engine's age and the crew's lack of competence the ship's first voyage was delayed for five weeks and further repairs were required at the end of it, resulting in the loss of a further 15 weeks. The defendants purported to terminate the contract so the claimants sued for beach of contract on the grounds that the defendant had no right to terminate; the defendants claimed that the claimants were in breach of a contractual condition.
>
> *Decision:* the term was innominate and could not automatically be construed as either a condition or a warranty. The obligation of 'seaworthiness' embodied in many charter party agreements was too complex to be fitted into one of the two categories. The term would be construed in the light of the actual consequences of the actual breach. The ship was still available for 17 out of 24 months. The consequences of the breach were not so serious that the defendants could be justified in terminating the contract as a result. The defendants were in breach of contract for terminating it when they did.

Activity 2 (10 mins)

A company contracts for the purchase of 200 mobile telephones 'immediately suitable for use in the UK'. Assume that this term is innominate. How would the court classify it if:

(a) The telephones supplied required tuning to particular frequencies, a task taking two minutes for each one?

(b) Use of the telephones supplied was illegal in the UK, and they could not be modified to make their use legal?

How did you arrive at that conclusion?

3 IMPLIED TERMS

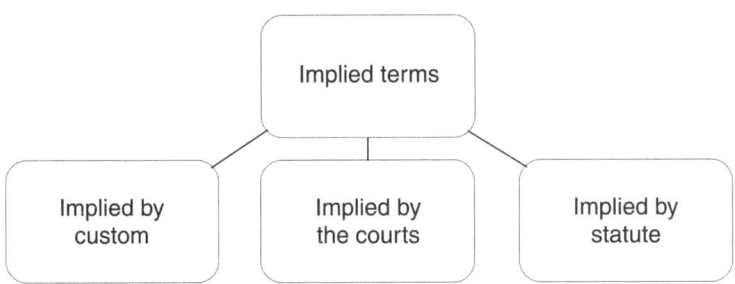

Additional terms of a contract may be implied by law.

3.1 Contractual terms implied by custom

The parties may be considered to enter into a contract subject to a custom or practice of their trade. For example, when a farm is let to a tenant it may be an implied term that local farming custom on husbandry and tenant rights shall apply: *Hutton v Warren 1836*. But any express term overrides a term which might be implied by custom.

> *Les Affreteurs v Walford 1919*
> A charter of a ship provided expressly for a 3% commission payment to be made on signing the charter. There was a trade custom that it should only be paid at a later stage. The ship was requisitioned by the French government before the charterparty began, and so no hire was earned.
>
> *Held:* an express term prevails over a term otherwise implied by custom. The commission was payable on hire.

3.2 Contractual terms implied by statute

Terms may be implied by statute. In some cases the statute permits the parties to contract out of the statutory terms (thus the terms of partnership implied by the Partnership Act 1890 may be excluded). In other cases the statutory terms are obligatory. The protection given by the Sale of Goods Act 1979 to a consumer who buys goods from a trader cannot be taken away from him.

For example you have probably seen notices in shops which state that the shop accepts no responsibility for potential problems. Such notices invariably also say 'Your statutory rights are not affected'. They are making it clear that the Sale of Goods Act cannot be disapplied.

3.3 Contractual terms implied by the courts

Terms may be implied if the court concludes that the parties intended these terms to apply and did not mention them because they were taken for granted or because they were inadvertently omitted. The court may then supply a further term to prevent the failure of the agreement and to implement the manifest intention of the parties. The contract is given 'business efficacy'. In such cases the 'officious bystander' test is applied; if an officious bystander had intervened to remind the parties that in formulating their

contract they had failed to mention a particular point they would have replied 'of course ... we did not trouble to say that; it is too clear'.

> *The Moorcock 1889*
>
> The owners of a wharf agreed that a ship should be moored alongside to unload its cargo. It was well known to both wharfingers and shipowners that at low tide the ship would ground on the mud at the bottom. At low tide the ship rested on a ridge concealed beneath the mud and suffered damage.
>
> *Held:* it was an implied term, though not expressed, that the ground alongside the wharf (which did not belong to the wharfingers) was safe at low tide since both parties knew that the ship must rest on it.

Terms will not be implied to contradict the express terms of the contract (see *Les Affreteurs* case in paragraph 3.1 above) nor to provide for events which the parties did not contemplate in their negotiations.

4 SPECIALIST TERMS

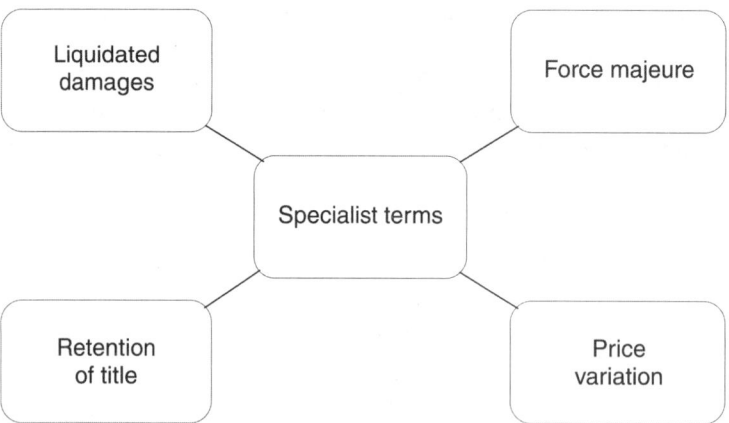

There are many specialist terms which are used in contract law, and the ones with which the Edexcel Guidelines are concerned tend to relate to specific business situations.

You need to be able to recognise them if used in assignments, and also appreciate their importance.

4.1 Force majeure

Force majeure clauses are also sometimes referred to as hardship clauses.

Definition

> **Force majeure clauses** are inserted into contracts, sometimes as a matter of routine, when the parties can foresee that difficulties are likely to arise but the parties cannot foresee their precise nature or extent.

This is especially common in the engineering or building trades.

The subject matter of force majeure clauses can range from the effect of an engineering component being unavailable, so that a contract cannot be completed in its current form, to such 'acts of God' as a ship sinking with all of the contract's necessary supplies on it.

4.2 Price variation clauses

As you have already seen, once a contract has been established, any change to the contract can only be achieved if both of the parties provide some form of fresh consideration, effectively therefore making an additional contract on top of the one which already exists.

Therefore it is difficult for one party to amend the price of the goods subject to the contract once it is in existence.

However, some contracts may include in them a clause stating that the price may be varied, and if this were in itself a contractual term, it would be valid. This type of clause is especially likely where the subject of the contract is some commodity whose price fluctuates, such as sugar, or where the contract is not likely to be fulfilled for some time.

A practical example is seen in the cases where people make hotel and other bookings to celebrate major events such as the Millennium or the Olympic Games a long time in advance (in many cases years in advance) but the price is not finally fixed until much closer to the event. The purchasers involved would have an opt-out clause to enable them not to buy, but if they did proceed with the contract they would be bound by the contractual price.

4.3 Retention of title clauses

The terms of a retention of title clause provide that where goods are sold, the seller can retain title to the goods (in other words still be the legal owner of them) until he is paid for them by the purchaser. The seller retains legal title even where possession of the goods passes to the seller. The advantage of this is that if the purchaser becomes insolvent, or for some other reason does not pay, the seller can recover the goods.

The goods, once recovered, may not be in as good condition as they were at the time of sale, and hence not worth as much, but it does give the seller some protection against losing all the value of his goods.

The Romalpa case

Retention of title clauses are often called Romalpa clauses after the first big case on the issue.

> *Aluminium Industrie Vaassen BV v Romalpa Ltd 1976*
> *The facts:* Romalpa purchased aluminium foil on terms that the stock of foil (and any proceeds of sale) should be the property of the Dutch supplier until the company had paid to the supplier all that it owed. Romalpa got into financial difficulties and a receiver was appointed. The receiver found that the company still held aluminium foil and proceeds of selling other stocks of foil, and had not paid its debt to the supplier. The receiver applied to the court to determine whether or not the foil and the cash were assets of the company under his control as receiver.

Decision: the conditions of sale were valid. The relevant assets, although in the possession of the company, did not belong to it. The receiver could not deal with these assets since his authority under the floating charge was restricted to assets of the company.

Further issues

The extent to which a Romalpa clause protects an unpaid seller depends to a great extent on the wording of the actual clause. A retention of title clause may be effective even though goods are resold or incorporated into the buyer's products so as to lose their identity if it expressly states that they can be used in these ways before title has passed: *Clough Mill Ltd v Martin 1985.*

Unless the clause expressly retains title even after resale or incorporation, the supplier is not entitled to a proportionate part of the sale proceeds of the manufactured product: *Borden (UK) Ltd v Scottish Timber Products Ltd 1979.* Where there is no express provision, resale or incorporation is conversion of the supplier's property but a third party will still get good title.

If the buyer resells the goods when there is an express provision allowing resale before title passes, the proceeds of sale are held by the buyer as trustee for the supplier.

One critical point about retention of title clauses is their communication. As with other contractual terms, they must be adequately communicated to the other party to the contract *before* the contract is entered into. A party who is expected to be bound by a retention of title clause must be aware of it prior to entering the contract, otherwise he cannot be expected to be bound by it.

Many companies include their retention of title clauses on their invoices. This is too late, as an invoice is not a pre-contractual document, and the contract has already been made by the time the invoice is sent to the purchaser. In order to be legally valid, a retention of title clause should be on a document such as an order form, or in a statement of terms sent out before the contract is agreed.

4.4 Liquidated damages clauses

To avoid calculations or disputes later over any amount payable, the parties may include in their contract a formula - **liquidated damages** for determining the damages payable for breach.

A genuine pre-estimate of loss

In construction contracts it is usual to provide that if the building contractor is in breach of contract by late completion a deduction is to be made from the contract price The formula will be enforced by the courts if it is '**a genuine pre-estimate of loss**'.

> *Dunlop Pneumatic Tyre Co Ltd v New Garage & Motor Co Ltd 1915*
> *The facts:* the contract imposed a minimum retail price. The contract provided that £5 per tyre should be paid if they were resold at less than the prescribed retail price. The defendant did sell at a lower price and argued that £5 per tyre was a 'penalty' and not a genuine pre-estimate of loss.
>
> *Decision:* in this case the formula was an honest attempt to agree on liquidated damages and would be upheld.

Compare this with:

> *Ford Motor Co (England) Ltd v Armstrong 1915*
> *The facts*: the defendant had undertaken not to sell the claimant's cars below list price, not to sell Ford cars to other dealers and not to exhibit any Ford cars without permission. A £250 penalty was payable for each breach.
>
> *Decision*: since the same sum was payable for different kinds of loss it was not a genuine pre-estimate of loss and was in the nature of a penalty.

Penalty clauses

Penalty clauses may look similar to liquidated damages clauses, but are designed to intimidate, rather than just to make good a loss.

A contractual term designed as a **penalty clause** to discourage breach is **void** and not enforceable. Relief from penalty clauses is an example of the influence of equity in the law of contract.

> *Bridge v Campbell Discount Co 1962*
> *The facts*: a clause in a hire purchase contract required the debtor to pay on termination, a sum which amounted to two thirds of the HP price and additionally to return the goods.
>
> *Decision*: this was a penalty clause and void since the creditor would receive on termination more than 100% of the value of the goods.

Activity 3   **(10 mins)**

A qualified accountant undertakes to prepare a client's tax return. The accountant then finds that the tax return form has been redesigned, and that his computer system cannot cope with the new design. Consider whether he could claim that there was no term in the contract stating that he should be able to prepare a return in the new form, and that he is therefore not obliged to do so.

5   EXCLUSION CLAUSES

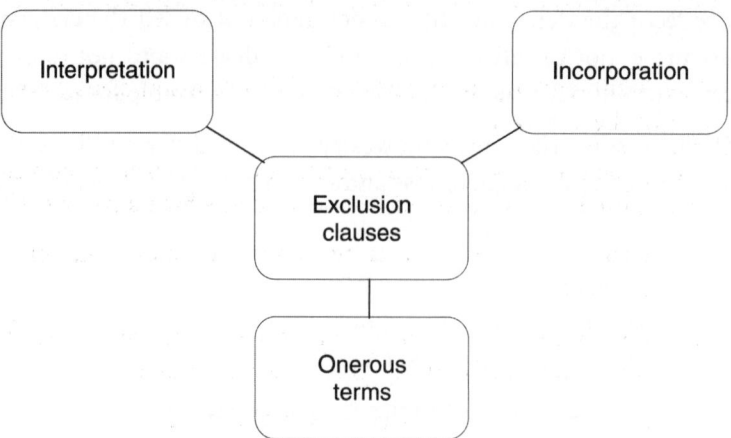

An exclusion (or exemption) clause is **a clause which seeks to release one of the parties from liability** should something go wrong with the contract.

If the parties negotiate their contract from positions of more or less equal bargaining strength and expertise, neither the courts nor Parliament have usually interfered. But there has been strong criticism of the use of exclusion clauses in contracts made between manufacturers or sellers of goods or services and private citizens as consumers, standard form contracts.

In such cases there may be great inequality. The seller puts forward **standard conditions** of sale which the buyer may not understand and must accept if he wishes to buy. In those conditions the seller may try to exclude or limit his liability for failure to perform as promised for breach of contract or negligence, or he may try to offer a 'guarantee' which in fact reduces the buyer's rights.   The law seeks to protect the individual from unfair exclusion clauses.

Requirements of an exclusion clause

The main limitations on exclusion clauses are now contained in the Unfair Contract Terms Act 1977 which applies to clauses excluding or restricting liability in contract or tort.

The Unfair Contract Terms Act is dealt with later in this chapter.

An exclusion clause which is not void by statute may still be ineffectual. The courts have generally sought to protect the consumer from the harsher effects of exclusion clauses in two ways.

(a)   An exclusion clause must be properly incorporated into a contract before it has any legal effect.

(b)   Exclusion clauses are interpreted strictly; this may prevent the application of the clause.

5.1   Incorporation of exclusion clauses

Uncertainty often arises over which terms have actually been incorporated into a contract. It is not enough for one party to claim that he possesses a set of draft terms; it

must be shown that any such terms were incorporated into the agreement between the parties when the agreement was formed. These rules apply to any contract and not just to exclusion clauses, although it is convenient to discuss them here, as many do concern exclusion clauses.

(a)   The document containing notice of the exclusion clause must be an integral part of the contract.

(b)   If the document is an integral part of the contract, a term may not usually be disputed if it is included in a document which a party has signed.

(c)   The term cannot be part of the contract unless put forward before the contract is made.

(d)   It is not a binding term unless the person whose rights it restricts was made sufficiently aware of it at the time of agreeing to it.

(e)   Onerous terms must be sufficiently highlighted.

Contractual documents

The courts will not treat an exclusion clause as a term of the contract unless the party affected by it was sufficiently informed of it when he accepted it. It must be shown that this document is an integral part of the contract and is one which could be expected to contain terms.

> *Chapelton v Barry UDC 1940*
> *The facts:* There was a pile of deck chairs and a notice stating 'Hire of chairs 2d (1p) per session of 3 hours'. The claimant took two chairs, paid for them and received two tickets which he put in his pocket. One of the chairs collapsed and he was injured. The defendant council relied on a notice on the back of the tickets by which it disclaimed liability for injury.
>
> *Decision:* the notice advertising chairs for hire gave no warning of limiting conditions and it was not reasonable to communicate them on a receipt. The disclaimer of liability was not binding on the claimant.

> *Thompson v LMS Railway 1930*
> *The facts:* An elderly lady who could not read asked her niece to buy her a railway excursion ticket on which was printed 'Excursion: for conditions see back'. On the back it was stated that the ticket was issued subject to conditions contained in the company's timetables. These conditions excluded liability for injury.
>
> *Decision:* the conditions had been adequately communicated and therefore had been accepted.

In the Chapelton case, the ticket was a mere receipt; in the Thompson case, it should have been obvious to a reasonable person that the ticket had contractual effect, as tickets of that kind generally contain contract terms.

Signed contracts

If a person signs a document containing a clause restricting his rights he is held to have agreed to the restriction even if he had not read the document. But this is not so if the party who puts forward the document for signature gives a misleading explanation of its legal effect.

L'Estrange v Graucob 1934
The facts: A sold to B, a shopkeeper, a slot machine under conditions which excluded B's normal rights under the Sale of Goods Act 1893. B signed the document without reading the relevant condition.

Decision: the conditions were binding on B since she had signed them. It was not material that A had given her no information of their terms nor called her attention to them. (Under the law as it now stands, some rights under the Sale of Goods Act 1979, which replaced the 1893 Act, may not be excluded.)

Curtis v Chemical Cleaning Co 1951
The facts: X took her wedding dress to be cleaned. She was asked to sign a receipt on which there were conditions by which the cleaners disclaimed liability for damage however it might arise. Before signing X enquired what was the effect of the document and was told that it restricted the cleaner's liability in certain ways and in particular placed on X the risk of damage to beads and sequins on the dress. The dress was badly stained in the course of cleaning.

Decision: the cleaners could not rely on their disclaimer since they had misled X as to the effect of the document which she signed. She was entitled to assume that she was running the risk of damage to beads and sequins only.

Activity 4 **(5 mins)**

A contract between P and Q includes a clause excluding P's liability in certain circumstances. When Q enquires as to the meaning of this clause, P replies that he does not wish to provide an oral interpretation, but that Q must read the clause for herself. Q reads the clause and signs the contract. P later seeks to rely on the exclusion clause, and Q claims that P should have interpreted the clause for her. The clause itself is not misleadingly phrased. Consider whether Q is likely to be able to prevent P from relying on the clause.

Prior information on terms

Many contracts are entered into without the parties signing a document. In such cases, exclusion clauses may be stated on notices or tickets. However, since the terms of the contract are fixed at the moment of acceptance of the offer, an exclusion clause cannot be introduced thereafter (except by mutual consent). Each party must be aware of an exclusion clause at the time of entering into the agreement if it is to be binding.

Olley v Marlborough Court 1949
The facts: A husband and wife arrived at a hotel and paid for a room in advance. On reaching their bedroom they saw a notice on the wall by which the hotel disclaimed liability for loss of valuables unless handed to the management for safe-keeping. The wife locked the room and handed the key in at the reception desk. A thief obtained the key and stole the wife's furs from the bedroom.

Decision: the hotel could not rely on the notice disclaiming liability since the contract had been made previously (when the room was booked and paid for) and the disclaimer was too late.

Complications can arise when it is difficult to determine at exactly what point in time the contract is formed so as to determine whether or not a term is validly included.

> *Thornton v Shoe Lane Parking Ltd 1971*
> *The facts:* X saw a sign saying 'Parking' outside the defendant's car park. He drove up to the unattended machine and was automatically given a ticket. He had seen a sign disclaiming liability for damage to cars before obtaining the ticket and when he received the ticket he saw that it contained words which he did not read. In fact these made the contract subject to conditions which, if he had looked hard enough in the car park, also excluded liability for injury. When he returned to collect his car (which had been stacked in a special machine) there was an accident in which he was badly injured.
>
> *Decision:* the contract was formed before he got the ticket (the offer was the 'Parking' sign; acceptance was parking his car so as to receive a ticket) so reference on the ticket to conditions was too late for the conditions to be included as contractual terms. (Note that since UCTA 1977 the personal injury clause would be void anyway.)

Previous dealings

An exception to the rule that there must be prior notice of the clause is where the parties have had consistent dealings with each other in the past, and the documents used then contained similar clauses: *J Spurling Ltd v Bradshaw 1956*.

If the parties have had previous dealings (not on a consistent basis) then the person to be bound by the exclusion clause may be sufficiently aware of it (as a proposed condition) at the time of making the latest contract. For this purpose it is necessary to show in a consumer contract that he actually knew of the condition; it is not sufficient that he might have become aware of it.

> *Hollier v Rambler Motors 1972*
> *The facts:* On three or four occasions over a period of five years H had had repairs done at a garage. On each occasion he had signed a form by which the garage disclaimed liability for damage caused by fire to customers' cars. On the latest occasion, however, he did not sign the form. The car was damaged by fire caused by negligence of garage employees. The garage contended that the disclaimer had by course of dealing become an established term of any contract made between them and H.
>
> *Decision:* the garage was liable. There was no evidence to show that H knew of and agreed to the condition as a continuing term of his contracts with the garage.

But in a commercial contract it is sufficient to show that, by a previous course of dealings, the other party has constructive if not actual notice of the term: *British Crane Hire Corporation Ltd v Ipswich Plant Hire 1974*.

> **Activity 5**   **(5 mins)**
>
> Customers of a self service shop take goods from the shelves and then walk down a corridor to a till. A conspicuous notice is hung across this corridor incorporating an exclusion clause into contracts for the purchase of goods from the shop. Could a customer claim that the exclusion clause was invalid because he had selected goods before seeing the notice?
>
> Why is this so?

5.2 Onerous terms

Where a term is particularly unusual and onerous it should be highlighted so that the attention of the other party is drawn to it when the contract is being formed. Failure to do so may mean that it does not become incorporated into the contract.

> *Interfoto Picture Library Ltd v Stiletto Visual Programmes Ltd 1988*
> *The facts:* Forty-seven photographic transparencies were delivered to the defendant together with a delivery note with conditions on the back. Included in small type was a clause stating that for every day late each transparency was held a 'holding fee' of £5 plus VAT would be charged. They were returned 14 days late. The claimants sued for the full amount of £3,782.50.
>
> *Decision:* the term was onerous and had not been sufficiently brought to the attention of the defendant. The court reduced the fee to 50p per transparency per day (one tenth of the contractual figure) to reflect more fairly the loss caused to the claimants by the delay.

5.3 Interpretation

In deciding what an exclusion clause means, the courts interpret any ambiguity against the person at fault who relies on the exclusion. This is known as the *contra proferentem* rule (against the person relying on it).

The contra proferentem rule

Liability can only be excluded or restricted by clear words. In particular, if the clause gives exclusion in unspecific terms it is unlikely to be interpreted as covering negligence on the part of the person relying on it unless that is the only reasonable interpretation.

> *Hollier v Rambler Motors 1972*
> The facts are as given in section 5.1. The garage disputed liability for fire damage to the claimant's car on the basis of a contractual term which stated that the company was not liable for damage caused by fire to customers' cars on the premises.
>
> *Decision:* as shown above, the term was not incorporated into the contract; as a matter of interpretation the disclaimer of liability could be interpreted to apply (a) only to accidental fire damage or (b) to fire damage caused in any way including negligence. It should therefore be interpreted against the

garage in the narrower sense of (a) so that it did not give exemption from fire damage due to negligence.

Alderslade v Hendon Laundry 1945
The facts: The conditions of contracts made by a laundry with its customers excluded liability for loss of or damage to customers' clothing in the possession of the laundry. By its negligence the laundry lost A's handkerchief.

Decision: the exclusion clause would have no meaning unless it covered loss due to negligence. It did therefore cover loss by negligence.

When construing an exclusion clause the court will also consider the main purpose rule. By this, the court presumes that the clause was not intended to defeat the main purpose of the contract.

Fundamental breach

There used to be some doubt on how far an exclusion clause could exclude liability in a case where the breach of contract was a failure to perform the contract altogether (a fundamental breach). In the case given below the House of Lords overruled some earlier decisions of the Court of Appeal and so the legal position is now reasonably clear.

Photo Productions v Securicor Transport 1980
The facts: Securicor agreed to guard the claimants' factory under a contract by which Securicor were excluded from liability for damage caused by any of their employees. One of the Securicor guards deliberately started a small fire which got out of hand and destroyed the factory and contents, worth about £615,000. It was contended (on the authority of earlier decisions of the Court of Appeal) that Securicor had entirely failed to perform their contract since they had not guarded the factory and so they could not rely on any exclusion clause in the contract.

Decision: there is no principle that total failure to perform a contract deprives the party at fault of any exclusion from liability provided by the contract. It is a question of interpretation of the exclusion clause whether it is widely enough expressed to cover total failure to perform. In this case the exclusion clause was wide enough to cover the damage which had happened. (As the fire occurred before the UCTA came into force in 1977 the Act could not apply here. But if it had done it would have been necessary to consider whether the exclusion clause was reasonable.)

Activity 6 **(5 mins)**

A road haulage company's standard conditions exclude liability for delays caused by factors beyond the company's control. Would this exclusion be interpreted to cover a delay due to a driver choosing to use minor roads because he found motorway driving boring, given that it is the company's policy never to interfere with drivers' choices of routes? Why?

6 UNFAIR CONTRACT TERMS LEGISLATION

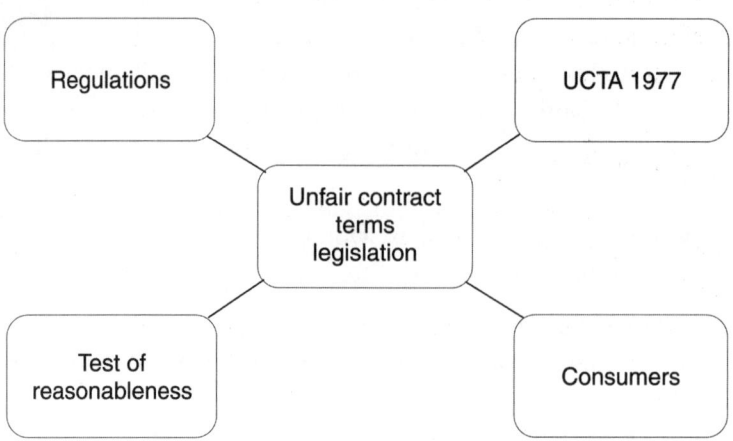

Before we consider the specific term of UCTA, it is necessary to describe how its scope is restricted.

(a) In general the Act only applies to clauses inserted into agreements by commercial concerns or businesses. In principle private persons may restrict liability as much as they wish.

(b) The Act does not apply to certain contracts, for example contracts relating to the creation or transfer of interests in land, contracts relating to company formation or securities transactions and insurance contracts.

6.1 Unfair Contract Terms Act 1977 (UCTA)

The Act uses two techniques for controlling exclusion clauses: some types of clauses are void, whereas others are subject to a test of reasonableness. The main provisions of the Act are as follows.

Avoidance of liability for negligence (s 2)

A person acting in the course of a business cannot, by reference to any contract term, restrict his liability for death or personal injury resulting from negligence. In the case of other loss or damage, a person cannot restrict his liability for negligence unless the term is reasonable. 'Negligence' covers breach of contractual obligations of skill and care, the common law duty of skill and care and the common duty of occupiers of premises under the Occupiers' Liability Acts 1957 and 1984.

Avoidance of liability for breach of contract (s 3)

The person who imposes the standard term, or who deals with the consumer, cannot, **unless the term is reasonable,**

(a) Restrict liability for his own breach or fundamental breach, or

(b) Claim to be entitled to render substantially different performance or no performance at all.

Unreasonable indemnity clauses (s 4)

A clause whereby one party undertakes to indemnify the other for liability incurred in the other's performance of the contract is void if the party giving the indemnity is a consumer, unless it is reasonable.

Sale and supply of goods (ss 6-7)

A consumer contract for the sale of goods, hire purchase, supply of work or materials or exchange of goods cannot exclude or restrict liability for breach of the conditions relating to description, quality, fitness for the purpose for which sold and sample implied by the Sale of Goods Act 1979 and the Supply of Goods and Services Act 1982. In a non-consumer contract these implied conditions may be excluded if the exclusion clause is **reasonable**. The implied condition as to title cannot be excluded in any contract.

Activity 7   **(5 mins)**

A contract for the sale of a washing machine to a consumer contains the following clause: 'The seller undertakes to repair any defects arising within the first 12 months free of charge, and the buyer shall accordingly not be permitted to return the machine if it does not work at the time of sale'. A consumer would normally have a statutory right to return the machine if it did not work at the time of sale. Consider whether this right has effectively been excluded by the clause.

6.2 Consumers (s 12)

A person deals as a consumer if:

    (a)   He neither makes the contract in the course of a business, nor holds himself out as doing so and

    (b)   The other party does make the contract in the course of a business and

    (c)   The goods are of a type ordinarily supplied for private use or consumption.

Where a business engages in an activity which is merely incidental to the business, the activity will not be in the course of the business unless it is an integral part of it and it will not be an integral part of it unless it is carried on with a degree of regularity.

> *R & B Customs Brokers Ltd v United Dominions Trust Ltd 1988*
> The claimants, a company owned by Mr and Mrs Bell and operating as a shipping broker, bought a second-hand Colt Shogun. The car was to be used partly for business and partly for private use.
>
> *Held:* this was a consumer sale, since the company was not in the business of buying cars.

6.3 Test of reasonableness (s 11)

The term must be fair and reasonable having regard to all the circumstances which were, or which ought to have been, known to the parties when the contract was made. The burden of proving reasonableness lies on the person seeking to rely on the clause. Statutory guidelines have been included in the Act to assist in the determination of

reasonableness although the court has discretion to take account of all factors. For example, for the purposes of ss 6 and 7, the court will consider the following.

(a) The relative strength of the parties' bargaining positions and in particular whether the customer could have satisfied his requirements from another source.

(b) Whether any inducement (such as a reduced price) was offered to the customer to persuade him to accept a limitation of his rights and whether any other person would have made a similar contract with him without that limitation.

(c) Whether the customer knew or ought to have known of the existence and extent of the exclusion clause (having regard, where appropriate, to trade custom or previous dealings between the parties).

(d) If failure to comply with a condition (for example, failure to give notice of a defect within a short period) excludes or restricts the customer's rights, whether it was reasonable to expect when the contract was made that compliance with the condition would be practicable.

(e) Whether the goods were made, processed or adapted to the special order of the customer.

Activity 8 (10 mins)

A contract under which a consumer buys a 20 volume encyclopaedia contains a clause excluding liability for defects not notified within a week of delivery. Two weeks after delivery, the buyer finds that several pages which should have been printed are blank. Will the seller be able to rely on the exclusion clause?

What is the reason for your answer?

6.4 Regulations

The Unfair Terms in Consumer Contracts Regulations (UTCCR) 1999, as updated by the Unfair Terms in Consumer Contracts (Amendment) Regulations 2001, replace the UTCCR 1994, which implemented an EC directive on unfair terms in consumer contracts. The regulations have created a three tier system for dealing with unfair terms in the UK: common law, Unfair Contracts Terms Act 1977, The Regulations 1999.

The Regulations apply to unfair terms in contracts concluded between a seller or supplier and a consumer. They do not apply to terms which reflect mandatory or statutory provisions in the UK, or the provisions or principle of international conventions to which the EC is a party.

Definitions

Consumer: any natural person who, in contracts covered by these Regulations, is acting for purposes which are outside his trade, business or profession.

Seller or supplier: any natural or legal person who, in contracts covered by these Regulations, is acting for purposes relating to his trade, business or profession, whether publicly owned or privately owned.

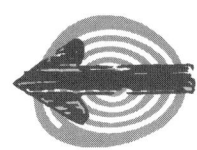

The concept of separate legal personality is covered in the law specialist units. All you need to be aware of is that in the eyes of the law entities such as companies can be regarded as 'persons' in their own right, quite independently of the individuals who own it.

Unfair terms

A contractual term which has not been individually negotiated (for example one in a standard form contract) shall be regarded as unfair if, contrary to the requirements of good faith, it causes a significant imbalance in the parties' rights and obligations arising under the contract, to the detriment of the consumer. A Schedule to the Regulations contains an indicative list of terms which may be regarded as unfair, for example:

- Terms which exclude or limit the liability of a seller in the event of death of a consumer resulting from an act or omission of that seller

- Terms requiring any consumer who fails to fulfil his obligation to pay a disproportionately high sum in compensation

- Terms obliging the consumer to fulfil all his obligations where the seller or supplier does not perform his

You can find these regulations at www.hmso.gov.uk, in the Statutory Instruments section. The regulations are 1999/2083. Review the schedule to the regulations to see all the potentially unfair terms listed there.

The unfairness of terms shall be assessed, taking into account the nature of the goods and services for which the contract was concluded and by referring to all the circumstances attending to the conclusion of the contract and all the other terms of the contract or of another contract on which it is dependent.

A term found to be unfair shall not be binding on the consumer although the contract shall continue in existence if it is capable of continuing without the unfair term. The Director General of Fair Trading or a named qualifying body, for example, the Financial Services Authority, may apply for an injunction to prevent the use of an unfair term drawn up for general use in contracts concluded with consumers.

Activity 9 (30 mins)

Find a business contract relating to your own responsibilities at work (eg for the purchase of office supplies, or a copy of your company's standard order form) or your homelife (eg your electricity supply contract). Examine it in detail and consider:

- Who drafted it?

- Is it a standard form contract?

- Why it is drafted the way it is.

- Whether you think any exclusion clauses would be effective.

NOTES

Chapter roundup

- If a purported contract omits an essential term, and gives no means for settling that term, there is no contract.

- Statements made in the course of negotiations may not become terms of a contract at all. They may only amount to representations.

- A condition is a term which is vital to a contract, and its breach allows the party not in breach to treat the contract as discharged. Breach of a warranty, on the other hand, only entitles the injured party to damages.

- Innominate terms can only be classified as conditions or warranties once the effects of their breach can be assessed.

- Some terms may be implied by law whereas others are so obvious that they are implied under the 'officious bystander' test.

- A force majeure clause can try to pre-empt the effect of a problem cropping up in the contract.

- Force majeure clauses are common in the building and engineering industries.

- Price variation clauses may be valid where the contract provides for it.

- Retention of title means that the seller of goods can retain ownership of them until they have been paid for by the purchaser.

- Liquidated damages are calculated by reference to a pre-agreed formula included in the contract.

- Exclusion clauses are not automatically illegal, but some such clauses are ruled out to prevent abuses of economic power by one party.

- Exclusion clauses must be properly incorporated into a contract at or before the time of acceptance, and must not be presented in a misleading manner.

- Exclusion clauses are interpreted strictly, against the person seeking to rely on them.

- The Unfair Contract Terms Act 1977 makes certain exclusion clauses void, and others void unless they are reasonable.

- The UTCCR 1999 defines what is meant by an unfair term.

Quick quiz

1   What is the difference between a representation and a contract term?

2   What is the difference between a condition and a warranty?

3   Explain the significance of an innominate term.

4   In what circumstances may additional terms, not expressed in the contract, nonetheless be implied as part of it?

5   When will a court treat an exclusion clause as void because the affected party was not properly informed?

PROFESSIONAL EDUCATION

6   What effect does the fact that parties have had previous dealings have on an exclusion clause?

7   If there is ambiguity in an exclusion clause, how does the court interpret the clause?

8   When may liability for negligence never be excluded?

9   What tests are applied to determine the reasonableness of an exclusion clause?

10   How does UCTA 1977 define a consumer?

Answers to quick quiz

1   A representation is something said before the contract. A term is something incorporated within the contract.

2   Condition: central to the contract so a breach causes the contract to fail

        Warranty: less important, so a breach does not cause the contract to fail

3   It can be interpreted as either a condition or a warranty, depending on the effects of the breach.

4   By custom
        By statute
        By the courts

5   Where it was not properly incorporated in the contractual documents.

6   If the previous dealings were consistent, the exclusion clause may be upheld.

7   Against the person trying to enforce the exclusion clause.

8   In cases of death or personal injury.

9   Relative strength of bargaining positions
        Inducements offered
        Knowledge of the exclusion clause
        Failure to observe a condition
        Special treatment of the goods

10   The consumer

        -   Is not acting in the course of a business
        -   The other party is acting in the course of a business
        -   The goods would normally be supplied for private use

Answers to activities

1   No: if there is no agreement, a definite price (£50,000) is automatically fixed.

2   (a)   A warranty
        (b)   A condition

        In the latter situation the buyer is being deprived of the whole benefit of the contract. In part (a) it is not an insurmountable problem.

3   No: it is an implied term that a qualified accountant can prepare a tax return in any form required by the Inland Revenue.

4   No: Q has not been misled.

PROFESSIONAL EDUCATION

NOTES

5   No: the exclusion clause was notified before the contract was made at the till.

6   No: the company could choose to control its drivers' choices of routes.

7   No: a consumer contract cannot exclude the statutory term that goods are fit for their purpose.

8   No: it is not reasonable to expect a consumer to find all printing defects in a 20 volume work within the first two weeks of use.

9   There is no specific answer to this activity.

Assignment 5   **(45 minutes)**

Brian was driving his car through Birmingham looking for a convenient car park. He noticed two car parks adjacent to each other where the car parking charges were identical. Whilst deciding which one to use he saw a notice displaying 'closed circuit television in operation' in the car park owned by 'Secure Car Parks Ltd'. He decided that he would park his car in that car park because of the additional security measures.

As he drove in, and before he had taken a ticket from the machine, he also saw another notice: 'Cars parked at owners' risk'. No responsibility whatsoever is accepted for any cars damaged or stolen, howsoever caused'.

When he returned to his car some three hours later he was annoyed to find that a car window had been smashed and his radio and cassettes had been stolen.

He immediately contacted the attendant to explain what had happened but the rather unhelpful attendant simply pointed to the notice by the entrance. Brian, admitting knowledge of the notice excluding liability, asked the attendant if he could look at a video recording from the cameras in the hope that he could identify the culprit. The attendant said that it was not possible to play a recording because the cameras had not worked for three months since they were struck by lightning.

Brian was astounded by this revelation and threatened legal action against the car park owners.

Advise Brian on any possible action(s) he may have and any defences that Secure Car Parks Ltd may have.

PART C

THE LAW OF TORT

Chapter 8 :
THE LAW OF TORT

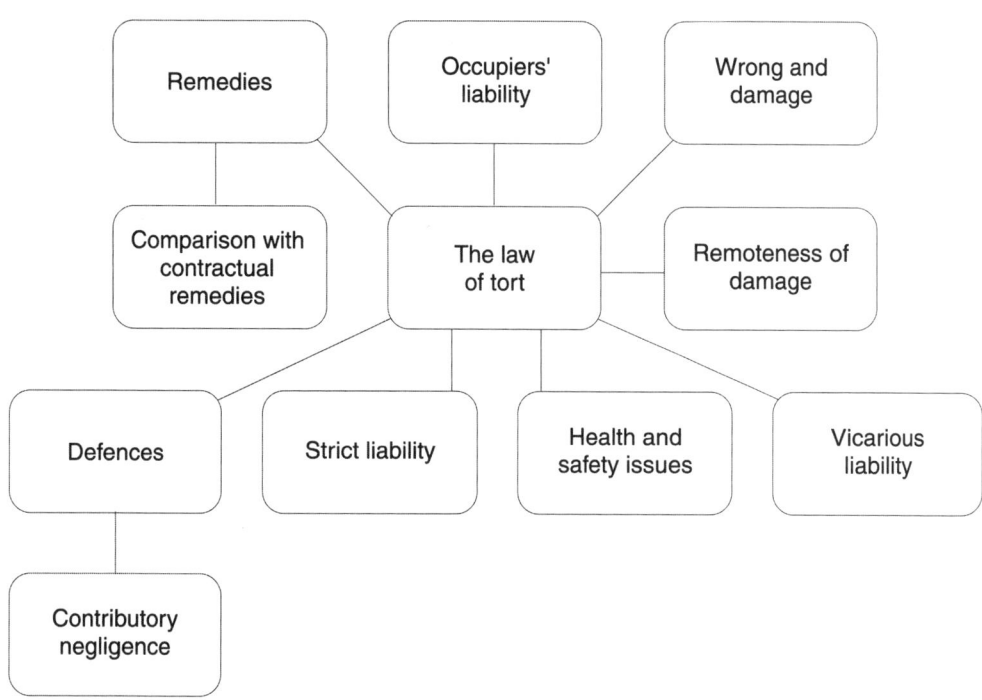

Introduction

There is no entirely satisfactory definition of tort. The principle is that the law gives various rights to persons, such as the right of a person in possession of land to occupy it without interference or invasion by trespassers. When such a right is infringed the wrongdoer is liable in tort. The law of tort is concerned really with a person's responsibility to others. It applies to both individuals and companies.

There is therefore a duty imposed by law to respect the legal rights of others. When a tort is committed the remedy is an action at common law for unliquidated damages (ie damages not established by a formula in a contract), which represent such compensation as the court may see fit to award. The principles of tort are based on rights, the related duty to respect them and compensation for infringement.

Tort is distinguished from other legal wrongs.

(a)   A **crime** is an offence prohibited by law. The state **prosecutes** the offender and **punishment** is by fine or imprisonment. A tort is a **civil wrong** and the person wronged **sues** in a civil court for compensation (or for an injunction against repetition).

(b)   **Breach of contract** and breach of trust are **civil wrongs**. It must be shown that the defendant was subject to the obligations of a contract or a trust and did not perform or observe those obligations. In tort no previous transaction or relationship need exist: the parties may be complete strangers.

Your objectives

In this chapter you will learn about the following.

(a) The significance of both wrong and damage;

(b) How damage is assessed for remoteness;

(c) When an employer may be responsible for a tort committed by an employee;

(d) The rule in Rylands v Fletcher;

(e) The main defences to an action in tort;

(f) The effect of contributory negligence;

(g) The main remedies for torts, and the types of damages which may be awarded;

(h) Health and safety issues.

1 WRONG AND DAMAGE DISTINGUISHED

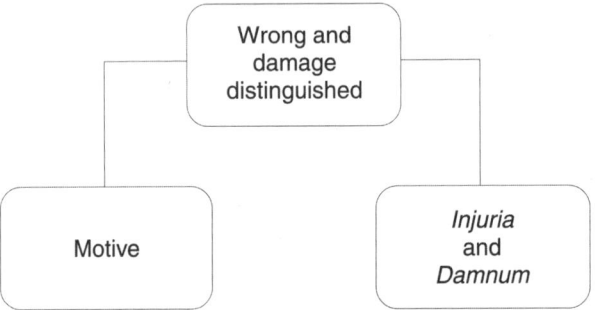

1.1 *Injuria and damnum*

When a claimant sues in tort claiming damages as compensation for loss, he must normally prove his loss. But the necessary basis of his claim is that he has suffered a wrong. If there is no wrong *(injuria)* for which the law gives a remedy, no amount of damage *(damnum)* caused by the defendant can make him liable. *Damnum sine injuria* (loss not caused by wrong) is not actionable.

In some torts it is necessary to establish both wrong and loss resulting from it; this is the rule in the tort of negligence. But in other cases, for example, trespass or libel, it is enough to prove that a legal wrong has been done and damages (possibly nominal in amount) may be recovered without proof of any loss *(injuria sine damno)*. Substantial damages may be awarded where the loss is serious, but difficult to quantify in money terms, as in cases of damage to reputation by defamation.

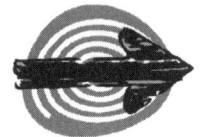

Negligence will be covered in the next chapter.

1.2 Motive

In tort, unlike crime, it is not usually necessary to prove anything about the defendant's state of mind. A good motive will not excuse a tortious act and a bad motive *(malice)* will not turn an innocent act into a tortious one. (There are a few exceptions such as the tort of *malicious prosecution* where there must be evidence of malice.)

Mayor of Bradford v Pickles 1895
The facts: P wished the Bradford Corporation to buy his land, adjoining the corporation's water reservoir, at a very high price. He sank a shaft on his land to divert the flow of subterranean water through it (as he was legally entitled to do). As a result less water flowed into the reservoir and it was discoloured. The corporation sued for an injunction, a court order to P to desist.

Decision: the action must fail. P was exercising his rights as a landowner and was not infringing any rights of the corporation. It was immaterial that the corporation had suffered loss and that P's express motive was to inflict loss.

Activity 1 (10 mins)

Tony plants trees in his garden. The roots remain on his land, but the trees soak up water from Peter's garden next door, thereby causing Peter's plants to wither. Is there *injuria*? Is there *damnum*?

2 REMOTENESS OF DAMAGE

When a person commits a tort with the intention of causing loss or harm which in fact results from the wrongful act, that loss or harm can never be too remote a consequence. Damages will be awarded for it.

2.1 *Novus actus interveniens*

If the sequence of cause and effect includes a new act (called a *novus actus interveniens*) of a third party or of the claimant, it may terminate the defendant's liability at that point: further consequences are too remote and he is not required to pay compensation for them. But where the intervening act is that of a third party who could be expected to behave as he did in the situation arising from the defendant's original wrongful act, the intervening act does not break the chain.

Scott v Shepherd 1773
The facts: A threw a lighted firework cracker into a crowded market. It landed on the stall of B who threw it away. It then landed on the stall of C who threw it away and it then hit D in the face and blinded him in one eye. D sued A.

Held: there was no break in the chain of causation from A's intentional wrongful act despite the fact that it was C who actually threw it so it hit D. A was liable to D.

2.2 Reasonable foresight

If the intervening act is that of the claimant himself and he acts unreasonably, for example, by taking an avoidable and foreseeable risk of injury to himself, that breaks the chain (or if it does not it may reduce his claim for loss because of his contributory negligence).

When there is a sequence of physical cause and effect without human intervention, the ultimate loss is too remote (so that damages cannot be recovered for it) unless it could have been reasonably foreseen that some loss of that kind might occur as a consequence of the wrong.

The Wagon Mound 1961

The facts: A ship (the *Wagon Mound*) was taking on furnace oil in Sydney harbour. By negligence oil was spilled onto the water and it drifted to a wharf 200 yards away where welding equipment was being used to repair another ship. The owner of the wharf at first stopped work because of the fire risk but later resumed working because he was advised that sparks from a welding torch were unlikely to set fire to furnace oil. Safety precautions were taken. A spark fell onto a piece of cotton waste floating in the oil and this served as a wick, thereby starting a fire which caused damage to the wharf. The owners of the wharf sued the charterers of the *Wagon Mound*, basing their claim on an earlier decision that damage caused by a direct and uninterrupted sequence of physical events is never too remote even though it could not reasonably be foreseen.

Decision: the claim must fail. The earlier decision was overruled and the reasonable foresight test was laid down. Pollution was the foreseeable risk: fire was not. This was a decision of the Privy Council on appeal from Australia and as such only a persuasive precedent for English courts. But as it was a decision of the most senior English judges, it is always applied in cases where the claim is for negligence.

Hughes v Lord Advocate 1963

The facts: Workmen left lighted paraffin lamps as a warning sign of an open manhole in the street. Two small boys took one of the lamps as a light and went down the manhole. As they clambered out the lamp fell into the hole and caused an explosion in which the boys were injured. Evidence was given that a fire might have been foreseen but an explosion was improbable.

Decision: the defendants were liable for negligence in leaving the lamps where they did. A risk of fire was foreseeable and the explosion must be regarded as 'an unexpected manifestation of the apprehended physical dangers'. It was not (as it was in the *Wagon Mound* case) damage of an entirely different kind.

Doughty v Turner Manufacturing Co 1964

The facts: An asbestos cement lid accidentally fell into a cauldron of sodium cyanide at a temperature of 800 degrees Centigrade. The intense heat caused a chemical change in the asbestos lid as a result of which there was an explosion. The claimant was injured by the eruption of molten liquid. The chemical reaction leading to the explosion was previously unknown to science.

Decision: a splash of sodium cyanide was foreseeable but a violent explosion was not. The result was unforeseeable as no one knew it could happen and therefore too remote.

In cases of physical injury which is more serious than would normally be expected because the plaintiff proves to be abnormally vulnerable, the defendant is liable for the full amount of injury done. This is the thin skull (or 'eggshell skull') principle: if A taps B on the head and cracks B's skull because it is abnormally thin, A is liable for the fracture.

> *Smith v Leech Braine & Co 1962*
>
> *The facts:* A workman was near a tank of molten zinc in which metal articles were dipped to galvanise them. One article was allowed to slip and the workman was burnt on the lip by a drop of molten zinc. The burn activated latent cancer from which he died three years later. His widow sued for damages.
>
> *Decision:* damages for a fatal accident would be awarded. Some physical injury (the burn on the lip) was a foreseeable consequence. The defendants must accept liability for the much more serious physical injury (cancer) caused by their negligence.

If the claimant suffers avoidable loss because his lack of resources prevents him from taking costly measures to reduce his loss, he may still recover damages for it: *Martindale v Duncan 1973*.

Activity 2   **(10 mins)**

A factory owner noticed that a machine was not running smoothly. She had heard of similar cases in which the increased vibration had led to small parts flying off and causing minor injuries, so she warned the workers to check that all such parts were secure and instructed them to carry on using the machine. The motor disintegrated and part of it broke through the casing and badly injured a worker, who then sued the factory owner. Why would the factory owner be unlikely to be able to rely on either The *Wagon Mound 1961* or *Doughty v Turner Manufacturing Co 1964* in her defence?

---

3   VICARIOUS LIABILITY

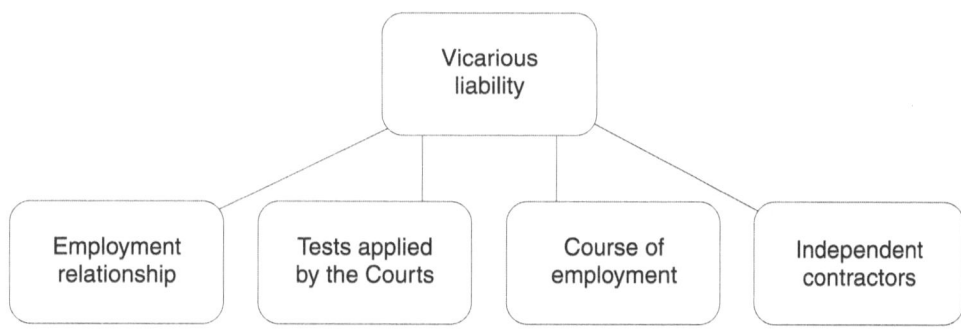

Definitions

Tortfeasor: a person who commits a tort,

Joint and several liability. This means that where one person commits a tort, another person may be liable jointly with the tortfeasor, or even separately on his own if the tortfeasor has disappeared.

A tortfeasor is always liable for his wrong. Others may be jointly and severally liable with him under the principle of **vicarious liability**. If, for example, a partner commits a tort either with the authority of the other partners or in the ordinary course of the firm's business, the other partners are liable with him.

The most important application of the principle of vicarious liability is to the **relationship of employer and employee.** It is often not worthwhile to sue the individual employee for damages since he is unable to pay them. The employer however has greater resources and may also have insurance cover.

To make the employer liable for a tort of the employee it is necessary that:

(a) there is the relationship between them of **employer and employee**; and

(b) the employee's tort is **committed in the course of his employment**.

3.1 Employment relationship

It is usually clear enough whether an employment relationship exists because of the formalities it involves (such as PAYE). Sometimes, however, it can be unclear whether a person is an employee and certain tests are applied by the courts in such circumstances to assess whether the employer has **control** over the way the employee performs his duties, whether the employer is **integrated** into the organisation and the **economic reality** of the situation.

3.2 Tests applied by the courts

The control test

Has the employer **control** over the way in which the employee performs his duties?

> *Mersey Docks & Harbour Board v Coggins & Griffiths (Liverpool) 1947*
> *The facts:* Stevedores hired a crane with its driver from the harbour board under a contract which provided that the driver (appointed and paid by the harbour board) should be the employee of the stevedores. Owing to the driver's negligence a checker was injured. The case was concerned with whether the stevedores or the harbour board were vicariously liable as employers.
>
> *Decision:* in the House of Lords, that the issue must be settled on the facts and not on the terms of the contract. The stevedores could only be treated as employers of the driver if they could control in detail how he did his work. But although they could instruct him what to do, they could not control him in how he operated the crane. The harbour board (as 'general employer') was therefore still the driver's employer.

The integration test

If the employee is so skilled that he cannot be controlled in the performance of his duties, was he appointed and assigned to his duties by the employer - was he **integrated** into the employer's organisation?

> *Cassidy v Ministry of Health 1951*
>
> *The facts:* The full-time assistant medical officer at a hospital carried out a surgical operation in a negligent fashion. The patient sued the Ministry of Health as employer. The Ministry resisted the claim arguing that it had no control over the doctor in his medical work.
>
> *Decision:* in such circumstances the proper test was whether the employer appointed the employee, selected him for his task and so integrated him into the organisation. If the patient had chosen the doctor the Ministry would not have been liable as employer. But here the Ministry (the hospital management) made the choice and so it was liable.

The multiple test

Is the employee working **on his own account**?

> *Ready Mixed Concrete (South East) v Ministry of Pensions & National Insurance 1968*
>
> *The facts:* The driver of a special vehicle worked for one company only in the delivery of liquid concrete to building sites. He provided his own vehicle (obtained on hire purchase from the company) and was responsible for its maintenance and repair. He was free to provide a substitute driver. The vehicle was painted in the company's colours and the driver wore its uniform. He was paid gross amounts (no tax etc deducted) on the basis of mileage and quantity delivered as a self-employed contractor. The Ministry of Pensions claimed that he was in fact an employee for whom the company should make the employer's insurance contributions.
>
> *Decision:* in such cases the most important test is whether the worker is working on his own account (the **entrepreneurial** test or **multiple** test). On these facts the driver was a self-employed transport contractor and not an employee.

Other factors

Other significant factors are as follows.

(a) Does the employee use his own **tools and equipment** or does the employer provide them?

(b) Does the alleged employer have the power to **select or appoint its employees,** and may it dismiss them?

(c) **Payment of salary** is, as mentioned above, a fair indication of there being a contract of employment. But there are exceptions. A person may still be an employee if he is paid no salary but derives his income solely from commission or tips. A person may receive a salary but not be an employee - for instance, Members of Parliament.

(d) Working for a number of different people is not necessarily a sign of self-employment. A number of assignments may be construed as a series of employments: *Hull v Lorimer 1994*.

In difficult cases, the court will also consider whether the 'employee' can **delegate** all his obligations (in which case, there is no contract of employment), whether there is restriction as to place of work, whether there is an obligation to work and whether holidays and hours of work are agreed.

> *O'Kelly v Trusthouse Forte Plc 1983*
>
> *The facts:* The employee was a 'regular casual' working when required as a waiter in the banqueting department of the Grosvenor Hotel. There was an understanding that he would accept work when offered and that the employer would give him preference over other more 'casual' employees, though they were all paid at the same rate. The industrial tribunal held that there was no contract of employment because the employer had no obligation to provide work and the employee had no obligation to accept work when offered. The Employment Appeal Tribunal however held that there had been a sequence of contracts of employment on each occasion.
>
> *Decision:* the Court of Appeal reinstated the finding of the industrial tribunal since it was a reasonable conclusion drawn from the particular facts. Whether there is a contract of employment is a question of law but it depends entirely on the facts of each case; here there was no 'mutuality of obligations' and hence no contract.

3.3 The course of employment

The employer is only liable for the employee's torts committed **in the course of employment**. Broadly the test here is whether the employee was doing the work for which he was employed. If so the employer is liable even in the following circumstances.

(a) The employee disobeys orders as to how he shall do his work.

> *Limpus v London General Omnibus Co 1862*
>
> *The facts:* The driver of an omnibus intentionally drove across in front of another omnibus and caused it to overturn. The bus company resisted liability on the ground that it had forbidden its drivers to obstruct other buses.
>
> *Decision:* the driver was nonetheless acting in the course of his employment. The company was liable to L who was injured in the accident.

> *Beard v London General Omnibus Co 1900*
>
> *The facts:* The same employer forbade bus conductors to drive buses. A bus conductor caused an accident while reversing a bus.
>
> *Decision:* the employer's instructions served to demarcate the limits of the conductor's duties. He was not, when driving, doing the job for which he was employed and so the employers were not liable to the person who was injured as a result of his actions.

General Engineering Services Ltd v Kingston and St Andrew Corporation 1988

The facts: Firemen were involved in a 'go-slow' policy in support of a pay claim and therefore took longer to reach a fire at the claimant's premises. The premises were destroyed as a result.

Decision: the employees were not employed to proceed to a fire as slowly as possible, thus their conduct amounted to an 'unauthorised act'.

(b) While engaged on his duties, the employee does something for his own convenience.

Century Insurance v Northern Ireland Road Transport Board 1942

The facts: A driver of a petrol tanker lorry was discharging petrol at a garage. While waiting he lit a cigarette and threw away the lighted match. There was an explosion.

Decision: the employer was liable since the driver was, at the time of his negligent act, in the course of his employment.

If the employer allows the employee to use the employer's vehicle for the employee's own affairs, the employer is not liable for any accident which may occur. There is the same result when a driver disobeys orders by giving a lift to a passenger who is injured.

Twine v Bean's Express 1946

The facts: In this case there was a notice in the driver's part of the van that the firm's drivers were forbidden to give lifts. The passenger was killed in an accident.

Decision: the passenger was a trespasser and in offering a lift the driver was not acting in the course of his employment. The driver was liable personally, not the company.

Contrast this with:

Rose v Plenty 1976

The facts: The driver of a milk float disobeyed orders by taking a 13 year old boy round with him to help the driver in his deliveries. The boy was injured by the driver's negligence.

Decision: the driver **was** acting in the course of his employment. The boy was not a mere passenger but was assisting in delivering milk. Therefore the company could be held liable for the driver's actions.

If the employee, acting in the course of his employment, defrauds a third party for his own advantage the employer is still vicariously liable.

Lloyd v Grace Smith & Co 1912

The facts: L was interviewed by a managing clerk employed by a firm of solicitors and agreed on his advice to sell property with a view to reinvesting the money. She signed two documents by which (unknown to her) the property was transferred to the clerk who misappropriated the proceeds.

Decision: the employers were liable. It was no defence that acting in the course of his employment the employee benefited himself and not them.

NOTES

Activity 3   **(10 mins)**

A research chemist employed by a drug company works in a laboratory in which, for safety reasons, all experiments involving the application of heat are forbidden. The chemist tries a reaction in which heat is spontaneously generated, and an explosion results, injuring other employees. Discuss whether the chemist acted in the course of his employment.

3.4 Independent contractors

If someone works for someone else and is not an employee, they are likely to be described as an **independent contractor**. Normally the person who engages an independent contractor is not liable for the latter's tortious acts. Generally, independent contractors are liable for their own torts. For example a builder may engage casual workers, such as electricians and plumbers, to work on specific projects. Such individuals are likely to be liable for their own wrongful acts.

However, a person who has work done not by his employee but by an independent contractor, such as a freelance plumber used by a builder, is vicariously liable for torts of the contractor in the following circumstances.

(a) The operation creates a hazard for users of the highway, as in repair of a structure adjoining or overhanging a pavement or road.

(b) The operation is exceptionally risky.

Honeywill & Stein v Larkin Bros 1934
The facts: Decorators who had redecorated the interior of a cinema brought in a photographer to take pictures of their work. The photographer's magnesium flare set fire to the cinema.

Decision: in commissioning an inherently risky operation through a contractor the decorators were liable for his negligence in causing the fire.

(c) The duty is personal. For example, an employer has a common law duty to his employees to take reasonable care in providing safe plant and a safe working system. If he employs a contractor he remains liable for any negligence of the latter in his work.

(d) There is negligence in selecting a contractor who is not competent to do the work entrusted to him.

(e) The operation is one for which there is strict liability (see below).

4   STRICT LIABILITY

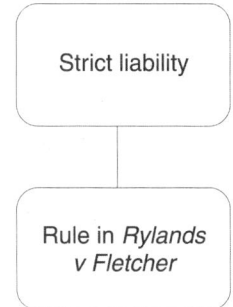

In many torts the defendant is liable because he acted intentionally or at least negligently. He may escape liability if he shows that he acted with reasonable care. That is essentially the position in the tort of negligence itself. But there are also torts which result from **breach of an absolute duty: the defendant is liable even though he took reasonable care**.

4.1   Rylands v Fletcher

The outstanding example of a tort of strict liability is the rule in *Rylands v Fletcher.*

'Where a person who, for his own purposes, brings and keeps on land in his occupation anything likely to do mischief if it escapes, he must keep it in at his peril, and if he fails to do so he is liable for all damage naturally accruing from the escape.'

> *Rylands v Fletcher 1868*
> *The facts:* F employed competent contractors to construct a reservoir to store water for his mill. In their work the contractors uncovered old mine workings which appeared to be blocked with earth. They did no more to seal them off and it was accepted at the trial that there was no want of reasonable care on their part. When the reservoir was filled, the water burst through the workings and flooded the mine of R on adjoining land.
>
> *Decision:* F was liable for the damage suffered by R, and the principle quoted above was laid down.

Activity 4   **(5 mins)**

A is the owner of a piece of land, and he knows that natural gas tends to accumulate in caverns under the land. Building works by A cause one of the caverns holding this gas to fracture, and the resulting escape of gas causes a fire on B's adjoining land. Why could B not sue A under the rule in Rylands v Fletcher?

BPP
PROFESSIONAL EDUCATION

5 DEFENCES TO AN ACTION IN TORT

In an action in tort the defendant may be able to rely on a defence applicable to the specific tort – such as justification in an action for defamation, or that he took reasonable care in an action for negligence. But those particular defences are not available in every tort action. There are, however, general defences which may be pleaded in any action in tort. Of these general defences the most important is consent.

5.1 Consent

Volenti non fit injuria (no wrong is done to a person who consents to it) is the maxim which describes consent as a defence in tort (sometimes abbreviated merely to *volenti*). It must however be true consent, which is more than mere knowledge of a risk, and also a consent which is **freely given**.

In some cases the plaintiff expressly consents to what would otherwise be a wrong. For example a hospital patient awaiting a surgical operation is asked to give his written consent to the operation. But more often the consent is merely the voluntary acceptance of a risk of injury.

> *ICI v Shatwell 1965*
> *The facts:* Two experienced shotfirers were working in a quarry. Statutory rules imposed on them (not their employer) a duty to ensure that all persons nearby had taken cover before a dangerous test was carried out. As their electric cable was too short they decided to carry out the test without taking cover before doing so. There was a premature explosion and both were injured. They sued the employer.
>
> *Decision:* they had consented to the risk. The employer was not liable since it had not been negligent nor had it committed or permitted a breach of statutory duty over safety procedures. The injured men were trained for their work and properly left to carry out safety procedures of which they were well aware.

Consent in taking a normal risk may be implied. A competitor in a boxing contest or a rugby match gives an implied consent to the risks incidental to the sports played fairly in accordance with its rules, even if the actual injury is exceptional. In the same way a spectator at a motor race or an employee engaged on inherently dangerous work, such as a test pilot of experimental aircraft or a steeplejack, is deemed to accept the inherent risks. But an employee, by accepting a job or continuing in it, does not consent to abnormal or unnecessary risks created by his employer merely because the employee is aware of them.

> *Smith v Baker & Sons 1891*
>
> *The facts:* S was put to work by B (his employer) in a position where heavy stones were swung over his head on a crane. Both S and B were aware of the risk. S was injured by a falling stone.
>
> *Decision:* S could recover damages. In working in circumstances of known risk he was not deemed to consent to the risk of the employer's negligence. This principle has been developed in later cases to impose on the employer a common law duty to provide a safe working system.

In other circumstances it has to be decided on the facts how far knowledge implies consent.

> *Morris v Murray 1990*
>
> *The facts:* The claimant and defendant spent all afternoon drinking together with another man. Despite the fact that the weather was poor, the two decided to go flying in a plane owned by the defendant, who piloted it. He took off downwind and uphill; in such conditions a different runway into the wind should have been used. The plane crashed, killing the defendant and severely injuring the claimant, who sued the defendant's estate. His administrators claimed *volenti non fit injuria* and/or contributory negligence on the part of the claimant.
>
> *Decision:* right from the beginning the drunken escapade was fraught with danger and, although drunk, the claimant knew what he was doing. It was very foreseeable that such an escapade would end tragically and so, by embarking on the flight, the claimant had implicitly waived his rights in the event of injury consequent on the deceased's failure to fly with reasonable care.

> *Kirkham v Chief Constable of Greater Manchester 1990*
>
> *The facts:* The deceased had hanged himself while in custody and his estate sued the police for negligence for failing to inform the prison authorities of the deceased's suicidal tendencies, contrary to official procedure.
>
> *Decision:* the defendants could not plead the defence of *volenti non fit injuria* because the claimant was suffering from a mental illness at the time of the suicide and therefore was not capable of consenting.

5.2 Rescue cases

A person who accepts a risk in order to effect a rescue does not lose his rights against the defendant if he is injured since his consent to the risk was constrained and not freely given. But the principle only applies when the risk is taken in order to safeguard others from the probability of injury for which the defendant is responsible.

Haynes v Harwood & Son 1935

The facts: The defendant's driver left his horse-drawn van unattended in a street. The horses bolted and a policeman (the claimant) ran out of the nearby police station to stop the horses since there was risk of injury to persons, including children, in the crowded street. He suffered injury in taking this action. The defendant pleaded volenti.

Decision the policeman (for the reasons given above) had not forfeited his claim by exposing himself to the risk.

Cutler v United Dairies 1933

The facts: The horse attached to an unattended horse-drawn van bolted into an empty field. The driver called for help and a spectator who responded was injured.

Decision: the spectator had consented to the risk. He was not impelled by the need to save others from danger. His claim was barred by his consent.

Activity 5   **(10 mins)**

A petrol tanker is supplying petrol to a filling station next to a busy road. A small fire starts on the forecourt, and a bystander picks up a fire extinguisher and goes to put it out. Because some petrol has been spilled, there is an explosion and the bystander is injured. If the bystander were to sue the petrol company, could the company plead *volenti non fit injuria*?

5.3   Unavoidable accident

Accident is a defence only if it could not have been foreseen nor avoided by any reasonable care of the defendant.

Stanley v Powell 1891

The facts: A member of a shooting party fired at a pheasant. A pellet glanced off a tree and injured a beater (the claimant).

Decision: the defendant was not liable as the ricochet and subsequent injury could not reasonably be foreseen.

5.4   Act of God

Act of God, which is an unforeseeable catastrophe, is a special type of unavoidable accident. This defence is rarely available.

5.5   Statutory authority

If a statute requires that something be done, there is no liability in doing it unless it is done negligently. If a statute merely permits an action it must be done in the manner least likely to cause harm and there is liability in tort, for nuisance, if it is done in some other way.

5.6 Act of State

If a person causes damage or loss in the course of his duties for the State, he may claim Act of State. But it is not a defence in any case where the claimant is a British subject or the subject of a friendly foreign power.

> *Buron v Denman 1848*
> *The facts:* D was captain of a British warship who had a general duty to suppress the slave trade. He set fire to a Spanish ship carrying slaves and released them. The Crown later ratified his act.
>
> *Decision:* neither D nor the Crown was liable.

5.7 Necessity

An act which causes damage may be intentional. If this is so, the defence of necessity may be raised, provided:

(a) that the act was reasonable (such as shooting a dog to prevent it worrying sheep), and

(b) either the act was done to prevent a greater evil or it was done to defend the realm.

5.8 Mistake

An intentional act done out of **mistake** may occasionally be defensible if it was reasonable. Such a case may be where a person makes a citizen's arrest in the reasonable and sincere belief that the claimant committed a crime.

5.9 Self defence

Similarly, **self defence** is a valid defence if the defendant acted to preserve himself, his family or his property, so long as the act was reasonable and in keeping with the nature of the threat. But if a blow is struck in response to mere verbal attack, there is no defence.

Activity 6 (5 mins)

A lorry is carrying mirrors which are standing upright. The whole cargo is covered by a tarpaulin. The tarpaulin breaks free, exposing one of the mirrors. The sun is reflected off this mirror into the eyes of the driver of another vehicle, which then crashes injuring a pedestrian. If the lorry owner is sued by the pedestrian, which defence should he put forward?

6   CONTRIBUTORY NEGLIGENCE

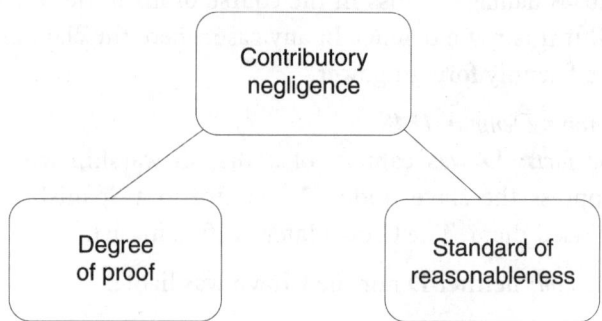

If the damage suffered as a result of negligence was partly caused by contributory negligence of the claimant his claim is proportionately reduced: Law Reform (Contributory Negligence) Act 1945.

6.1   Degree of proof

The defendant need not prove that the plaintiff owed him a duty of care. It is sufficient if part of the damage was due to the plaintiff's failure to take reasonable precautions to avoid a risk which he could foresee. If a motorcyclist, injured in a crash caused by the negligence of another driver, suffers avoidable hurt by failure to wear a crash helmet (which is compulsory), that is contributory negligence (*O'Connell v Jackson 1971*), which will reduce damages by 15% if injury would have been less had the helmet been worn and 25% if it would not have happened at all: *Froom v Butcher 1976*. So too is failure of a front seat passenger in a car to use a seat belt. The test of contributory negligence is what caused the damage, not what caused the accident.

6.2   Standard of reasonableness

There is however a standard of reasonableness. Mere failure to take a possible precaution or even thoughtlessness or inattention are not contributory negligence, unless there is a failure to do what a prudent person should do to avoid or reduce a foreseeable risk. If the plaintiff is a workman working at a monotonous task or in factory noise which may dull his concentration, due allowance is made in determining whether he is guilty of contributory negligence. A child of any age may be guilty of contributory negligence, but in deciding whether he has been negligent the standard of reasonable behaviour is adjusted to take account of his inexperience.

> *Yachuk v Oliver Blais 1949*
> *The facts:* A boy of nine bought petrol from a garage stating falsely that his mother's car had run out of petrol down the road. It was supplied in an open margarine tub. The boy (and his friend of seven who accompanied him) wished in fact to play Red Indians. They set fire to the petrol and the elder boy was badly burnt. The garage pleaded contributory negligence by the boys.
>
> *Decision:* the garage was negligent in selling the petrol in this way. There was no evidence that the boys realised the danger of what they did and so it was not a case of contributory negligence.

Activity 7 (10 mins)

A factory has its own electrical generator. The building containing the generator is left unlocked so as to allow rapid access in the event of fire, but there is a notice on the door which reads (in full): 'High voltage. Trained electricians only'. A child of ten is negligently allowed by his parents to play near the building. The child enters the building, suffers an electric shock and is injured. To what extent could the building's owner plead contributory negligence to reduce damages payable to the child?

---

7 REMEDIES IN TORT

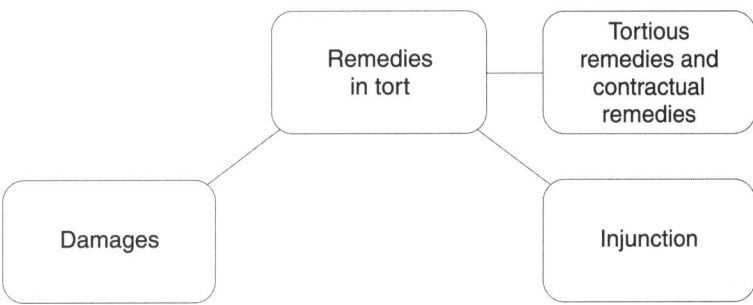

7.1 Damages

The amount of damages is based on the principle of compensating the claimant for his financial loss and not of punishing the defendant for his wrong. But there are several categories of damages related to the circumstances.

(a) **Ordinary (compensatory) damages** are assessed by the court as compensation for losses which cannot be positively proved or ascertained, and depend on the court's view of the nature of the claimant's injury.

(b) **Special damages** are those which can be positively proved, such as damage to clothing or cars.

(c) **Exemplary damages** or **aggravated damages** are intended to punish the defendant for his act, and to deter him and others from a similar course of action in the future. These damages are only rarely awarded. They are sometimes awarded in newspaper libel cases.

(d) **Nominal damages** are given where the claimant has suffered injury but has suffered no real damage (as in trespass to land without damage to that land).

7.2 Injunction

Injunction is an **equitable remedy** given by the court which requires an individual to refrain from doing a certain act, or orders him to do a certain act. There are two types of injunction.

(a) An **interlocutory injunction** is awarded before the hearing of an action so as to preserve the status quo. The claimant enters into an undertaking to pay the defendant for any loss arising out of the granting of the injunction.

(b) **A perpetual injunction** is granted after the full hearing and continues until revoked by the court.

7.3 Tortious remedies and contractual remedies

In most situations, a claimant will bring a case under **either** the law of contract or the law of tort, depending on the precise circumstances. If, however, the situation enables the claimant to bring a case under either, he may prefer to claim a tortious remedy as being more advantageous.

For example, Zed engages Bee to paint the exterior of his house for £2,000. Therefore they have a contract, the value of which is £2,000. During the course of the work, Bee negligently causes one of his ladders to crash through Zed's window and cause £10,000 worth of damage to a valuable painting. In such a situation it could be better for Zed to sue in tort, in order to recover the value of the loss, rather than to sue for breach of contact, for which damages would be limited to the value of the contract, £2,000.

In some situations, the same event can easily give rise to more than one legal liability. A road accident can lead to proceedings for crime, tort and even in contract, for example if the driver involved is a hired chauffeur. Bad professional advice may give rise to liability both in tort and in contract.

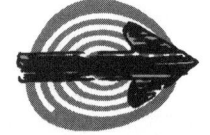

We shall discuss bad professional advice (negligent mis-statement) in the next chapter.

8 OCCUPIERS' LIABILITY

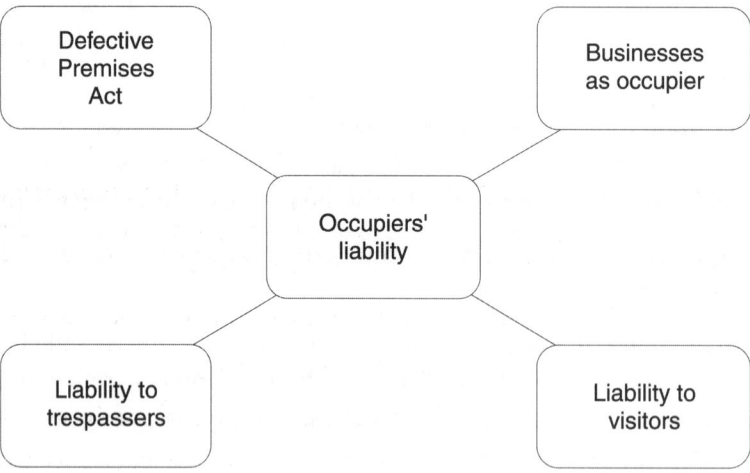

8.1 Businesses as occupier

One area of the law of tort which can potentially have a significant impact on businesses is occupiers' liability for damage or injury caused to people coming on to their premises.

An occupier of premises is any person (not necessarily the owner) who has control or possession of them. Occupation may be shared by two or more persons.

8.2 The liability to visitors

By statute (Occupiers' Liability Acts 1957 and 1984) an **occupier** owes a duty ('a common **duty of care**') to all **visitors** to the **premises** and must take such precautions as are necessary to make the premises reasonably safe for the purpose for which the visitor is permitted to enter them.

An occupier of premises is the person who has control of the premises. Ownership alone is not sufficient to constitute occupancy. In *Wheat v Lacon & Co Ltd 1966* it was held that the owners of a public house, which was managed by a manager, were nevertheless occupiers of it because of the degree of control they exercised over it.

Definition of a visitor

    (a)   A person who enters the premises with the actual or implied permission (or invitation) of the occupier

    (b)   A person such as a health inspector who has a legal right of entry

A person who enters to do business with the occupier is deemed to have implied permission although he may in fact not wish to see the visitor - as an example, a casual call by a sales representative hoping to sell his products to the occupier would make him a visitor. But there is no duty of care to a visitor who, after entering the premises, **exceeds the limits of the permitted purpose,** say by straying into parts of the building unconnected with his visit; he then becomes a trespasser.

Premises include not only land and buildings, but also fixed and moveable structures. Case law suggests that this definition is wide enough to include a mechanical digger, scaffolding and a lift.

The duty of care may vary with the visitor. An occupier is entitled to assume that lawful visitors will display ordinary prudence while on his premises.

    (a)   If the visitor is a specialist, for example a technician called in to do repairs, he is deemed to be aware of special risks incidental to his calling (eg no liability for the death by carbon monoxide poisoning of two sweeps called in to close a hole in a boiler chimney: *Roles v Nathan 1963)*.

    (b)   If he is a child, a higher standard of care is imposed on the occupier.

The occupier may discharge his duty to visitors as follows.

    (a)   **By taking reasonable measures,** such as repair work, to eliminate a hazard. He is not responsible for faulty work of an independent contractor, brought in to do specialist work. But he should inspect it. Thus an occupier will not be liable for the unsafe state of a lift due to negligence of the specialist firm employed to repair it but he remains liable when a school cleaner leaves slippery ice on a step (not a specialist task).

    (b)   **By giving warnings** where a warning is enough to enable the visitor to be reasonably safe. A visitor who ignores a warning may be consenting to the risk or may be guilty of contributory negligence. But a warning is not a sufficient precaution in some cases. It depends on the facts.

The occupier may in theory limit his liability to visitors on his premises by contract. But any such exclusion or limitation is restricted by the Unfair Contract Terms Act 1977 which among other provisions renders void a 'notice given to persons general'

purporting to exclude or restrict liability for death or personal injury resulting from negligence. The position of employees is protected by the Health and Safety at Work Act 1974 and related statutes and regulations.

8.3 Occupier's liability to trespassers

The Occupiers' Liability Act 1984 has replaced the common law rules governing the duty of occupiers of premises to persons other than visitors. Prior to 1984, the occupier's duty to trespassers was to act with common sense and humanity. This required all the surrounding circumstances to be considered, for example the seriousness of the danger, the type of trespasser likely to enter, and in some cases the resources of the occupier.

There is no satisfactory definition of 'trespasser'. It may include the innocent as well as the malicious. Broadly speaking it is a person who knows he does not intend communication with the occupier or anyone else on the premises.

> *British Railways v Herrington 1972*
>
> *The facts:* The local management of British Rail were aware that children gained entry to an electrified railway line through a broken-down fence which divided the line from land open to the public. British Rail merely reported the matter to the police but did not repair the fence. A child of six was injured on the line.
>
> *Decision:* the occupier's duty must be set by reference to the particular circumstances of the trespassers. A warning may be sufficient for an adult but it falls short of the duty of common humanity owed to a child to safeguard it from accessible and tempting perils on the occupier's land.

The main provisions of the 1984 Act are set out below.

Duty owed

The occupier owes a duty in the following circumstances.

(a) He is aware of the danger or has reasonable grounds to believe that it exists

(b) He knows or should know that someone is in (or may come into) the vicinity of the danger

(c) The risk is one against which he may reasonably be expected to offer that person some protection

Duty broken

The duty is to take such care as is reasonable in all the circumstances to see that the person to whom a duty is owed does not suffer injury on the premises by reason of the danger.

Damage

The occupier can only be liable for injury to the person. The Act expressly provides that there can be no liability for loss or damage to property.

Warnings

The duty may be discharged (in appropriate cases) by taking reasonable steps to give warning of the danger.

The 1984 Act does not significantly change the common law, although it does weight the balance more heavily against the occupier. It is therefore unlikely that Herrington's case would be decided differently under the Act and the outcome of other cases will still be difficult to predict.

A person using a right of way across land is neither a licensee nor an invitee and is therefore not a visitor. The occupier of the land is under no liability to users of the right of way for failure to keep it in good repair: *McGeown v Northern Ireland Housing Executive 1994*. Thus the 1984 Act applies to entrants other than trespassers.

8.4   Defective Premises Act 1972

This Act imposes on landlords a general liability, say to tenants' visitors, arising from a landlord's failure to repair the premises. It also imposes a statutory obligation on those who provide dwellings (landlords, builders, developers, local authorities etc) to ensure that each dwelling is fit for habitation. Furthermore, any work done (where a dwelling house is not built under an NHBC guarantee) must be carried out in a workmanlike or professional manner using proper materials A vendor of a house has similar duties towards a buyer and other persons reasonably expected to be affected.

Actions arising under the 1972 Act lie in tort. S 1 of the Act imposes 'strict liability' regarding fitness for habitation while the duty imposed on landlords under s 3 requires proof of negligence on the part of the defendant.

9   HEALTH AND SAFETY ISSUES

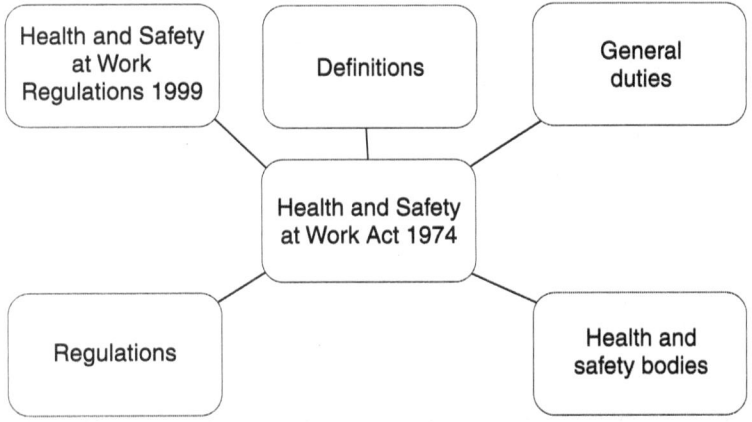

9.1   Introduction

The Edexcel Guidelines make specific reference to 'health and safety issues' in the context of tortious liability of employers. Much of health and safety is now covered by detailed legislation, and this applies to 'persons at work', so protects both employees and independent contractors.

There is a wealth of legislation and codes of practice on health and safety at work, which is often industry specific. We are going to look at some of the more general legislation in detail.

Much of the law relating to health and safety in the UK is derived from the EC, and many of the regulations we shall mention implement EC directives on these issues.

Statutory references in this section are to the Health and Safety at Work Act 1974 unless otherwise noted

9.2 Health and Safety At Work Act 1974: Definitions

In this section, we are going to look at the duties employers have to 'persons at work' and 'persons other than persons at work' under the Health and Safety at Work Act 1974.

Section 1 of Part I of the Act states:

The provisions of this Part shall have effect with a view to:

(a) Securing the health, safety and welfare of **persons at work**

(b) Protecting **persons other than persons at work** against risks to health and safety arising out of or in connection with the activities of persons at work

(c) Controlling the keeping and use of explosive or highly flammable or otherwise dangerous substances, and generally preventing the unlawful acquisition, possession and use of such substances

9.3 'Persons at work' and 'Persons other than persons at work'

As you will see in the following sections, the Act sometimes refers to employees and sometimes refers to others. The Act encompasses a wide variety of people to whom the employer may have responsibility as regards health and safety.

Definition

> **'Persons at work'.** The Act does not define this term, but does define 'work' as 'work as an employee or a self-employed person'. This means that 'persons at work' appears to cover both categories. It is not restricted to persons at work for the employer, so appears to mean anyone who comes within the scope of the employer while undertaking their own work. This therefore would include employees, independent contractors, visitors who are visiting for business purposes (for example, suppliers or professional advisers).
>
> **'Persons other than persons at work'** appears to mean any persons, extending to the general public.

9.4 'Reasonably practicable'

As you will also see in the following sections, the Act frequently uses the terms 'as far as is reasonably practicable'. It does not define what is meant by 'reasonably practicable' so this is a matter for the courts to consider as and when cases are brought under the Act.

Judges have determined that an employer must do what 'any reasonable employer' would have done. As a minimum, this means complying with the law, relevant Codes of Practice and Guidance notes.

As we shall see later, such Codes of Practice and guidance notes are issued by the Health and Safety Executive. There are a substantial number of such codes, and they can be extremely industry specific, so there is a significant burden on an employer to be up to date with the relevant guidance.

9.5 General duties

The Act contains a number of duties that we will look at in this section. We shall look at some of the more specific duties, such as the duties of landlords who are not the employer in considerably less detail than the specific duties of employees and employers to each other. However, ensure you are at least **aware** of all the general duties in this section.

The Act provides that it is a **criminal offence** for persons to fail to discharge a duty imposed by sections 2 to 7 or to contravene section 8 or 9.

9.6 General duties of employers to their employees: s2

There is a key, overriding duty owed by employers to their employees, which is: 'It shall be the duty of every employer to ensure, so far as is reasonably practicable, the health, safety and welfare at work of all his employees': s2(1).

As discussed above, employers must, as a minimum, follow law and relevant codes of practice.

Section 2 also identifies a number of matters which that duty extends to in practice, although these do not preclude other matters covered by the general duty in s2(1). These matters are that the employer ensures that:

- Plant and systems of work are provided and maintained so as to be safe and without risks to health.

- Arrangements are made so as to ensure safety and absence of risks to health in the use, handling, storage and transport of articles and substances

- He provides such information, instruction, training and supervision necessary to ensure health and safety of employees at work

- He maintains places of work, and access to and from such places, in such a condition as to ensure that they are safe and without risks to health

- The working environment provided and maintained is safe, without risks to health and has adequate facilities and arrangements for employee welfare at work

An employee has a duty to prepare a written policy on health and safety at the workplace: s2(3). He is also required to consult with employee representatives in making arrangements that assist him and his employees co-operating to ensure that the workplace is safe.

9.7 General duty of employers and self-employed to persons other than their employees: s3

Employers and those who are self-employed have a duty to ensure that the business is conducted in such a way as ensures that people not in his employment are not exposed to risks to their health and safety: s3.

9.8 General duty of persons concerned with premises to persons other than their employees: s4

This section states that persons who are responsible for non-domestic premises where others (who are not their employees) work should take measures to ensure that the premises and all means of access and exit from the premises are safe and without risks to health.

9.9 General duty of manufacturers etc as regards articles and substances for use at work: s6

This section imposes duties on people who manufacture articles for use at work to ensure that they are safe to so use.

9.10 General duty of employees at work: s7

This important section looks at the corresponding duty that employees have to their employers in relation to health and safety at work.

Section 7 states that:

'It shall be the duty of every employee while at work

(a) To take reasonable care for the health and safety of himself and of other persons who might be affected by his acts or omissions at work, and

(b) As regards any duty or requirement imposed on his employer or any other person by or under any relevant statutory provisions, to co-operate with him so far as is necessary to enable that duty or requirement to be performed or complied with.'

It is important that you note that the employee has a duty here to three groups of people:

- **Himself** (an employee must take care of his own health and safety at work)

- **Other persons** affected by his acts/omissions at work (that is, both fellow employees and any other persons affected by his work, perhaps visitors, or the public)

- **His employer** (whose requirements in relation to health and safety he must obey)

9.11 Duty not to interfere with or misuse things provided pursuant to certain provisions: s8

People must not intentionally or recklessly interfere with items provided for health and safety reasons. Examples might include letting off fire extinguishers or items in a first aid box.

9.12 Duty not to charge employees for things done or provided pursuant to certain specific requirements: s9

Employers must not charge employees if they are obliged to provide additional equipment (for example, goggles or anti-glare screens for computer screens) to comply with Health and Safety Regulations.

10 HEALTH AND SAFETY BODIES

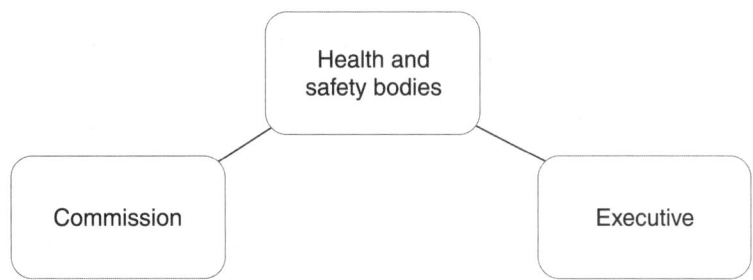

The 1974 Act provided that the Health and Safety Commission and the Health and Safety Executive should be set up. The Commission is a policy making body and the Executive is the enforcement body. Both are non-governmental bodies that nonetheless have significant connections with the government.

10.1 The Health and Safety Commission (HSC)

The Commission is a body with a Chairman appointed by the Secretary of State and between 6 and 9 appointed members. When appointing the members, the Secretary of State must consult employers' organisations, employees' organisations and local authority associations.

The HSC exists to:

- Assist and encourage others to further the purposes of the Act

- Carry out research related to health and safety at work and publish the results and encourage others to carry out research

- Provide information and training and advisory services in connection with health and safety at work

- Submit proposals to the Secretary of State for future regulations in connection with health and safety

- In general terms, the HSC furthers the work of the Secretary of State in relation to health and safety

The HSC is also empowered to set up enquiries into accidents at work.

10.2 The Health and Safety Executive (HSE)

The Executive is a body with three members, a Director General (appointed by the HSC with the approval of the Secretary of State) and two other members (appointed by the HSC in consultation with the Director General and the Secretary of State).

The HSE exists to:

- Carry out investigations as required by the HSC
- Act as a delegate for the HSC when required
- To give effect to HSC directions

The general operations division of the HSE is divided into 'directorates' in which most of the inspectors work, such as

- Field operations directorate (split into 7 sectors and the railway industry, it also has an occupational health and environment unit and a safety unit)

- Nuclear safety directorate (responsible for regulating nuclear safety)

- Hazardous installations directorate (concerned with petroleum industries, diving, sites where chemicals are used/stored or explosives are manufactured, pipelines and mining)

11 REGULATIONS

Section 15 of the Health and Safety at Work Act 1974 confers the right on the Secretary of State to make regulations and codes of practice in relation to health and safety. A substantial number of regulations have been passed under this section. We are going to look in detail at the Health and Safety at Work Regulations 1999, but so that you are aware of some of the legislation that has been passed, we shall list some here.

11.1 Examples

The following are examples of Regulations that have been passed under the authority of s15 of the Health and Safety at Work Act 1974. Many implement EC directives.

- The Classification of Hazards, Information and Packaging Regulations 1999

- The Confined Spaces Regulations 1997

- The Control of Substances Hazardous to Health Regulations 1999

- The Electricity at Work Regulations 1989

- The Health and Safety (Display Screen Equipment) Regulations 1992

- The Lifting Operation and Lifting Equipment Regulations 1998

- The Management of Health and Safety at Work Regulations 1999 (see paragraph 5)

- The Manual Handling Regulations 1992

- The Noise at Work Regulations 1989

- The Personal Protective Equipment Regulations 1992

- The Provision and Use of Workplace Equipment Regulations 1998

- The Working Time Regulations 1998 (as amended)

- The Workplace (Health Safety and Welfare) Regulations 1992

Activity 8 (30 mins)

You should be able to find the above regulations on the Stationery Office's website (www.hmso.gov.uk). This has a search engine that should enable you to find the Regulations by entering key words. Look up some of these regulations in order to get an impression of the requirements they impose on employers.

> ### Activity 9 (30 mins)
>
> Using the same website address given in activity 1, look specifically this time at the Workplace (Health, Safety and Welfare) Regulations 1992 (SI No 3004 in 1992). These regulations include some specific requirements which employers should comply with, such as temperature and lighting. Including these two issues, what requirements do the Regulations impose on employers?

> ### Activity 10 (30 mins)
>
> Using the same website address given in activity 1, look specifically at the Working Time Regulations 1998 (SI No 1833 in 1998). These regulations deal with the amount of time for which it is safe for workers to work. What general duties do the regulations impose upon employers and what rights do the regulations give to employees?

12 HEALTH AND SAFETY AT WORK REGULATIONS 1999

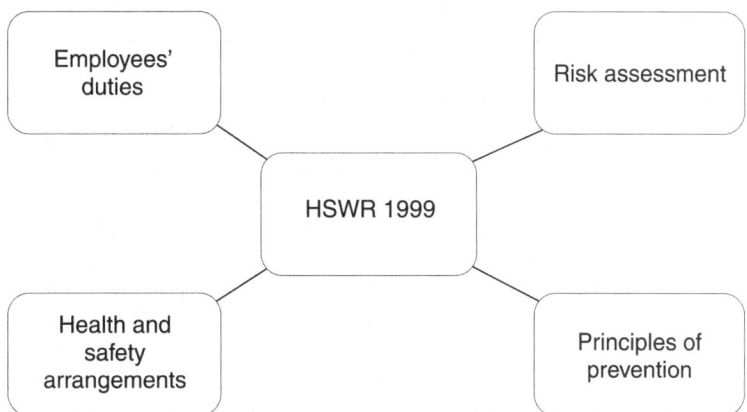

In the rest of this Chapter we shall look at the requirements of the Health and Safety at Work Regulations 1999. These replace the Regulations of the same name from 1992, which implemented EC directives numbers 89/391 and 91/383. The 1999 regulations, in addition, implement EC directives on pregnant workers and young people at work.

Statutory references in this section are to Health and Safety at Work Regulations 1999

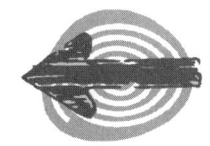

12.1 Risk assessments

One of the most significant requirements of the Health and Safety at Work Regulations 1999 is the requirement on employers and self-employed people to make assessments of the health and safety risks which employees and others are exposed to as a result of the undertaking. The risk assessment is designed to show the employer what requirements and prohibitions he must comply with.

The risk assessment itself must be reassessed if there is reason to believe that it is no longer valid or there has been a significant change.

If the employer employs five or more persons, the significant findings of the assessment must be recorded, as must any group of people who are particularly at risk.

Young people

The regulations identify young people as being people who are particularly at risk and imposes specific requirements on the employer in relation to them. A young person is classed as someone between the ages of 16 and 18. The employer must take particular note of:

- The inexperience, lack of awareness and immaturity of young persons

- The fitting out and layout of the workplace and the workstation

- The nature, degree and duration of exposure to physical, biological and chemical agents

- The form, range and use of work equipment and the way in which it is handled

- The organisation of processes and activities

- The extent of health and safety training provided or to be provided to young persons, and

- Risks from agents, processes and work listed in Directive 94/33/EC

12.2 Principles of prevention

Having conducted a risk assessment, the employer must implement procedures, as will be discussed in paragraph 12.3. The Regulations require the employer to implement those procedures on the basis of the EC's principles of prevention, as set out in Directive 89/391.

GENERAL PRINCIPLES OF PREVENTION

(a) Avoiding risks

(b) Evaluating risks that cannot be avoided

(c) Combating the risks at source

(d) Adapting the work to the individual, especially as regards the design of workplaces, the choice of work equipment and the choice of working and production methods, with a view, in particular, to alleviating monotonous work and work at a pre-determined work-rate and to reducing their effect on health

(e) Adapting to technical progress

(f) Replacing the dangerous by the non-dangerous or the less dangerous

(g) Developing a coherent overall prevention policy which covers technology, organisation of work, working conditions, social relationships and the influence of factors relating to the working environment

(h) Giving collective protective measures priority over individual protective measures, and

(i) Giving appropriate instructions to employees

12.3 Health and safety arrangements

The general requirement to make health and safety arrangements is found in section 5:

'Every employer shall make and give effect to such arrangements as are appropriate, having regard to the nature of his activities and the size of his undertaking, for the effective planning, organisation, control, monitoring and review of the preventative and protective measures': s5(1) HSWR 1999.

Where there are five or more employees, the arrangements made must be recorded.

Procedures

There are various procedures that an employer must consider:

- Health surveillance, where appropriate
- Appointment of competent persons to assist (this is mandatory)
- Implement procedures for areas of serious and imminent danger areas

Information

Employers are required to give information to their employees on:

- The risks identified by the assessment
- The preventative and productive measures taken
- Procedures for serious and imminent danger areas

Considering capabilities

When appointing competent persons from amongst his employees to assist in heath and safety issues, the employer must give consideration to the capability of the employees chosen.

Special cases

The regulations go on to consider the employer's duties to persons who may be at particular risk for specific reasons. Young persons have already been mentioned above. The regulations also refer to the requirement to consider health and safety issues specifically in relation to new or expectant mothers, and also the requirement on employers to advise temporary workers of health and safety policies in force at the undertaking.

12.4 Employees' duties

Lastly, we shall consider the duties that the Health and Safety at Work Regulations 1999 put on employees, which are contained in Section 14.

Employees are required to use machinery or dangerous substances **in accordance with training** they have received **and** in accordance with **the instructions they have been given** by the employer.

An employer is also required to inform

- The employer
- Anyone else charged with health and safety duties in the organisation

Of any serious and imminent dangers to health and safety.

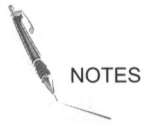

FOR DISCUSSION

What policies and procedures does your employer have in place in respect of health and safety? Are there any significant health and safety risks in the place where you work, to your knowledge? Have you been given a summary of the health and safety risk assessment carried out at your place of work? What did you think of it?

Chapter roundup

- A tort is a civil wrong arising from a general duty rather than from a contractual relationship.

- If a claimant has suffered damage but no legal wrong has been done, he will not succeed in his action. If a legal wrong has been done but no damage has been suffered, damages may be awarded in some cases, but they may be only nominal.

- In most torts, the claimant need not show that the defendant acted maliciously, only that he acted voluntarily.

- Damages will only be awarded for loss which is not too remote from the actions of the defendant. Chains of causation may be broken by the actions of others, or may become too tenuous when the consequences go beyond what could reasonably have been foreseen. However, the thin skull principle may allow damages to be awarded for unexpected damage.

- An employer is liable for torts committed by his employees in the course of their employment. An employee may be acting in the course of his employment even if he disobeys his employer's orders. Vicarious liability can also arise for the torts of independent contractors.

- The rule in *Rylands v Fletcher* defines a tort of strict liability, in which reasonable care is no defence. It covers the escape of anything brought onto the defendant's land and likely to do mischief if it escapes, but it does not cover things naturally on the land.

- Consent of the claimant is usually a defence to an action in tort, but someone who acts to save others does not consent to the risk involved in the rescue. Other defences include unavoidable accident, act of God, statutory authority, act of State, necessity, mistake and self defence.

- The main remedies for torts are damages (which are generally intended to compensate rather than to punish) and injunctions. Damages may be reduced to take account of contributory negligence by the claimant.

- An occupier owes a duty of care to all visitors to his premises, and to a certain extent to trespassers.

- The Health and Safety at Work Act 1974 puts a requirement on employers and self-employed to consider and protect the health and safety of persons at work and persons other than persons at work.

- S 2: General duties of employers to employees

- S 3: General duties of employers (self employed to persons other than employees

- S 4: General duty of persons concerned with premises to persons other than their employees

- S 6: General duty of manufacturers as regards articles/substances for use at work

- S 7: General duty of employees at work

- S 8: Duty not to interfere with/misuse things provided under regulations

- S 9 Duty not to charge employees for things done pursuant to regulations

- Employers general duty (s 2) is to ensure the health and safety of employees (as far as is reasonably practicable).

- Employees must take care for their health and safety of themselves and other persons and they must obey employers' health and safety requirements.

- The Health and Safety commission and Executive were set up to oversee health and safety in the UK.

- Many regulations have been issued under the authority of s 15 of the Act.

- The most key recent regulations are the Health and Safety at Work Regulations 1999.

- The regulations require employers to conduct health and safety assessments and then to implement procedures in response to the assessments.

- The employer must pay particular regard to persons who may be at high risk, for example, young persons and expectant mothers.

- Employees must use any equipment used at work in accordance with training and instructions given by the employer.

Quick quiz

1   What is a tort?

2   Distinguish wrong from damage, and identify the factors which must be present for there to be liability in tort.

3   How may remoteness of damage affect a claim in tort?

4   What two factors must be present for an employer's vicarious liability to be established?

5   When is a person liable for the torts of his independent contractor?

6   What is the rule in Rylands v Fletcher?

7   What does *volenti non fit injuria* mean?

8   When will the defence of necessity be effective?

9   What happens if the court finds that there was contributory negligence on the part of the claimant?

10 Describe the different types of damages which may be awarded.

11 What is a visitor in the context of the Occupiers' Liability Acts?

12 Who does an employer have responsibility to in relation to health and safety?

13 What are the general duties given in the 1974 Act?

14 What is the Health and Safety commission?

15 Name 5 sets of regulations made under the authority of s 15.

16 What matters must an employer consider when conducting a risk assessment in relation to young persons?

17 What are the employees' duties under the Health and Safety at Work Regulations 1999?

Answers to quick quiz

1   A tort is the infringement of someone else's rights

2   Wrong is breach of a legal duty. Damage is a loss suffered by the claimant. Usually both are required.

3   If the damage is too remote, the claimant will not be able to claim a remedy.

4   Employer-employee relationship
    Tort is committed in the course of employment.

5   Where the operation is hazardous, risky, personal.

6   The rule of strict liability.

7   No wrong is done to a person who freely consents to it.

8   If the act was reasonable and was done to prevent a greater wrong.

9   Damages will be proportionately reduced.

10 Ordinary
    Special
    Exemplary
    Nominal

11   A person who enters the premises with the actual or implied permission of the occupier, and a person with a legal right of entry.

12   'Persons at work' and 'persons other than persons at work'.

13   S 2: Employers to their employees
      S 3: Employers/self employed to others
      S 4: Persons concerned with premises to users
      S 6: Manufacturers of articles for use of work
      S 7: Employees
      S 8: Not to interfere with articles provided for health and safety
      S 9: Employer not to charge employee for health and safety items.

14   A body formed to encourage persons to further the provisions of the 1974 Act.

15   See the list given

16   Their inexperience/immaturity/lack of awareness

      The fitting out of the workplace/station

      The nature, degree and duration of exposure to physical, biological, chemical agents

      The form, range, use of work equipment/way in which it is handled

      The organisation of processes/activities

      The extent of health and safety training provided

      Risk from agents, processes, work listing in Directive 94/33

17   To use machinery etc in accordance with training/instructions given by the employer.

Answers to activities

1   There is damnum but no injuria. There is not therefore an actionable tort.

2   It was reasonably foreseeable that the part of the machine would break loose. The harm caused by large parts is of the same type as that caused by smaller parts.

3   It can be argued that the employee was doing the work for which he was employed, ie chemical experiments. Therefore the employer would be liable for the injuries. This follows cases such as *Limpus v London General Ombibus Co* and *Rose v Plenty*.

4   A did not bring the gas onto his land.

5   No: the bystander acted to prevent injury to other persons.

6   Unavoidable accident.

7   Not at all: the parents' negligence is irrelevant, and the child was too young to understand the risk.

8   This will depend on which regulations you have looked at.

9   The employer is required to ensure that every workplace complies with the regulations in respect of maintenance, ventilation, temperature, lighting, cleanliness, waste, dimensions/space, seating, floors and traffic routes, falls, falling objects, windows etc, doors, escalators, sanitary conveniences, washing facilities, drinking waters, accommodation for clothing/changes, facilities to rest/eat meals

10　Employers are required to take 'all reasonable steps' to ensure that employees don't work more hours than the time limits specified.

Employees are entitled to rest periods:

- 11 hours in every 24 hours
- 24 hours in every 7 days
- A break for every 6 hours worked consecutively

They are also entitled to 4 weeks paid annual leave.

Assignment 6   (1 ½ hours)

(a) It is settled law that an employer is vicariously liable for the negligence of his employee committed in the course of the latter's employment. How do the courts determine in such cases:

(i) Whether the tortfeasor was an employee

(ii) Whether the employee was acting in the course of his employment at the time of committing the tort?

Illustrate your answer from decided cases.

(b) Usha owns a derelict church which is currently being renovated and converted into a leisure complex by Buildco.

One evening Russell attempts to climb over the high wall surrounding the church in order to have a look around the site. In so doing, he tears his jacket and cuts his arm on a rusty barbed-wire fence laid around the top of the wall.

On the day following Russell's injury, Kylie, a local authority buildings inspector, visits the site to inspect Buildco's work. She is injured by a tile which falls from the roof of the church.

Advise Russell and Kylie on any claims they may have in the law of tort.

PART D

NEGLIGENCE

Chapter 9 :
NEGLIGENCE

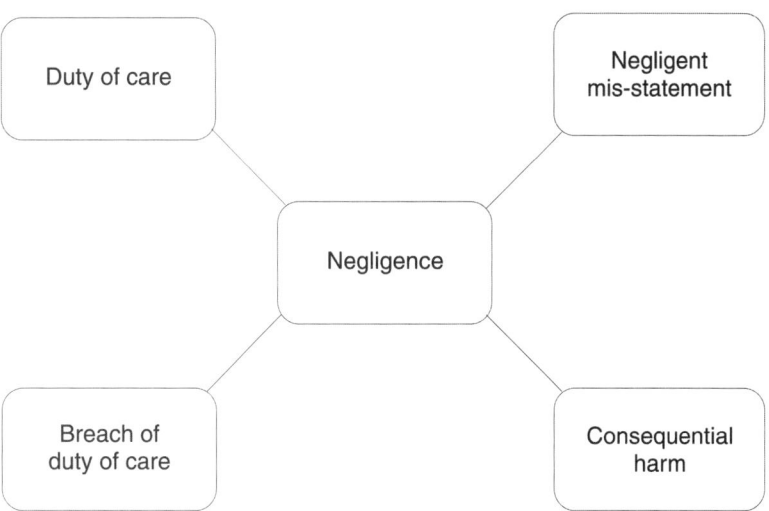

Introduction

As we saw in the previous chapter, many torts may be committed by mere carelessness rather than intentionally. In modern times the law has developed a tort of **negligence**, which is liability for a failure to take proper care to avoid inflicting foreseeable injury. It has become the most important and far-reaching of modern torts and is of particular relevance to businesses.

To succeed in an action for negligence the claimant must prove the following three things.

(a) The defendant owed him a **duty of care** to avoid causing injury to persons or property.

(b) There was a **breach** of that duty by the defendant.

(c) In **consequence** the claimant suffered injury, damage or (in some cases) **financial loss**.

Your objectives

In this chapter you will learn about the following:

(a) What must be proved in an action for negligence;

(b) The extent to which a duty of care may be owed;

(c) The extent to which nervous shock is actionable;

(d) What constitutes reasonable care;

(e) When *res ipsa loquitur* may be invoked;

(f) The main cases on negligent misstatement.

1 DUTY OF CARE

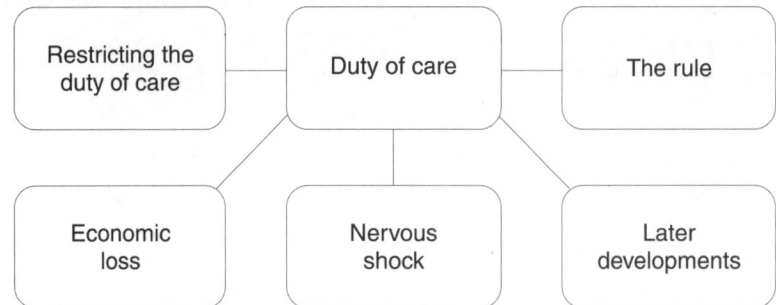

In the famed case of *Donoghue v Stevenson* the House of Lords ruled that a person might owe a duty of care to another person with whom he had no contractual relationship at all.

1.1 The rule

Donoghue v Stevenson 1932
The facts: A purchased from a retailer a bottle of ginger beer for consumption by A's companion B. The bottle was opaque so that its contents were not visible. B drank part of the contents of the bottle and topped up her glass with the rest. As she poured it out the remains of a decomposed snail emerged from the bottle. B became seriously ill. She sued C, the manufacturer, who argued that as there was no contract between himself and B he owed her no duty of care and so was not liable to her.

Decision: C was liable to B. Every person owes a duty of care to his 'neighbour', to 'persons so closely and directly affected by my act that I ought reasonably to have them in contemplation as being so affected'. In supplying polluted ginger beer in an opaque bottle the manufacturer must be held to contemplate that the person who drank the contents of the bottle would be affected by the consequences of the manufacturer's failure to take care to supply his product in a clean bottle.

1.2 Later developments

This narrow doctrine has been much refined in later cases. For any duty of care to exist, three points must be proved (as stated in *Anns v London Borough of Merton 1977*).

(a)   There must be a sufficient **relationship of proximity** or neighbourhood between the parties (defendant and claimant).

(b)   The defendant should be able **reasonably to foresee** that carelessness on his part may damage the claimant.

(c)   The law should allow that duty to **result in liability**. In particular, liability for the acts of independent third parties has been restricted.

The comments made in *Anns* suggest that objective foreseeability leads automatically to a duty of care and that a defendant who satisfies the foresight test is therefore liable unless there are reasons (such as public policy) why he should not be liable. In *Murphy v Brentwood DC 1990*, a case with facts similar to *Anns*, the House of Lords seems to have overruled its own decision on the earlier case, and the test of liability has been tightened, both by this case and by the *Caparo* case (see below). The *Murphy* case suggests that a duty of care will be based upon proximity, a principle similar to that in *Donoghue v Stevenson* itself.

The decision in *Caparo Industries plc v Dickman 1990* (which is discussed in detail later in the chapter) has also cast doubt on whether a single general principle of negligence can provide a practical test which may apply to every situation. In particular, the concepts of foreseeability or 'neighbourhood' are little more than convenient labels to attach to different specific situations before the court which, on detailed examination, it recognises as giving rise to a duty of care.

Activity 1   **(5 mins)**

Which of the following elements must be present for a duty of care to exist?

1   There must be a sufficient relationship of proximity between defendant and claimant

2   It must be reasonable that the defendant should foresee that damage might arise from his carelessness

3   The claimant must have acted in good faith and without carelessness

4   It must be just and reasonable for the law to impose liability

A   1 and 2 only
B   3 and 4 only
C   1, 2 and 3 only
D   1, 2 and 4 only

1.3 Restricting the duty of care

In any given case, if a reasonable man could have foreseen the consequences then a duty of care may be owed; whether it has actually arisen or not depends on the facts. The duty may be restricted or ignored completely in the following circumstances.

(a)   A person is not normally liable for the acts of third parties unless they were under his control. In an employment relationship, where there is control by the employer, the latter normally has vicarious liability for the acts of his servants done in the course of their employment.

(b)   Certain persons involved in judicial process are immune from all civil action, particularly judges, lawyers and jurors during a trial. Arbitrators are immune when they act in that capacity, as are valuers acting as arbitrators or quasi-arbitrators.

(c)   A person may be liable for omission, such as where an accountant carelessly leaves out part of his report, but a duty of care rarely arises from an obligation to take positive action which has not been taken.

Activity 2   **(5 mins)**

Consider the reasons why a barrister acting as an advocate in legal proceedings should be immune from being sued in negligence.

There is generally no duty to take care to prevent third parties from doing damage: mere foreseeability of damage is not enough.

Perl v Camden LBC 1983

The facts: Thieves entered an empty house owned by the defendant and broke through from there into the adjacent property, stealing a number of valuable items.

Decision: because there was no special relationship by which the house owner could control the acts of the thieves, no duty of care arose to the claimants.

But if the defendant is in control of third parties he has a duty of care in the exercise of that control.

Home Office v Dorset Yacht Club 1970

The facts: DY's property was damaged by a number of boys who escaped at night from a young offenders' institution. The escape was due to lack of care by the guards for whom the Home Office was responsible.

Decision: the Home Office was vicariously liable for the negligence of its staff as it owed a duty of care to persons whose property it could be foreseen might be damaged if the boys escaped.

1.4 Economic loss

One of the most uncertain areas in the law on negligence is how far and in what circumstances there is liability for financial (usually called 'economic') loss, if it is not the direct consequence of physical damage caused by negligence. The most common example of economic loss is where a person who has suffered physical damage makes a claim for loss of business profits while the damage is put right.

But in the last 25 years successful claims have been made for loss of profits both in cases where the root cause was physical damage and in cases where no actual physical damage occurred at all.

Ross v Caunters 1980

The facts: A solicitor gave negligent advice to a testator and drew up a will carelessly. A gift to the claimant (an intended beneficiary) failed as a result.

Decision: the solicitor owed a duty of care to beneficiaries since it was reasonably foreseeable that they would be damaged by negligent advice. The beneficiary could therefore sue for loss since he was actually in mind when the solicitor drew up the will.

If the courts can identify a special relationship 'akin to contract' between claimant and defendant, a claim for loss of profits may succeed. This case is generally regarded as exceptional.

Junior Books v Veitchi Co Ltd 1983

The facts: The defendants were sub-contractors engaged to lay a floor in the claimant's factory. Their contract was with the main contractor, not with the claimant. The floor was defective and had to be replaced (pure economic loss, as the only damage was to the product itself).

Decision: the defendants owed the claimants a duty of care. They were not producing goods for an unknown consumer; they were working for a particular person whose identity was known and who was relying on their skill and judgement as flooring contractors.

The special nature of the *Junior Books* case has been stressed in subsequent decisions, which have reverted to the award of damages for economic loss only where that loss is attached to physical loss.

> *Muirhead v Industrial Tank Specialities Ltd 1986*
> *The facts:* The claimants, wholesale fish merchants, purchased lobsters in the summer with the intention of selling them at Christmas when prices were higher. The pumps which they purchased to oxygenate the water were inadequate. The lobsters died.
>
> *Decision:* the death of the lobsters was reasonably foreseeable and this loss was recoverable. The additional losses were purely economic and were not recoverable.

Activity 3   **(5 mins)**

As a security measure, A installs lights outside his house. The house of B, his neighbour, is thereby illuminated, and B expresses his gratitude to A for choosing a security measure which benefits both of them. A later removes the lights without warning B, and the night after he does so B's house is burgled. Could B sue A?

1.5 'Nervous shock'

The claimant may claim compensation for nervous shock caused by the defendant's negligent act. Typically the claimant has suffered a reaction when they have witnessed an accident in which a close relative is injured. Compensation will not be awarded for mere grief or distress: the claimant must prove a definite and identifiable psychiatric illness.

Nervous shock is dealt with separately from ordinary physical damage because it has been perceived as a potential area for a vast litigation and therefore particular rules have developed. A duty of care is not owed to everyone who may in fact be affected by the defendant's act.

There is a duty of care not to cause nervous shock by putting a person in fear of his own safety *Dulieu v White & Sons 1901*, or in fear for the safety of his children *Hanbrook v Stoke Bros 1925*, or by making him an actual witness to an act of negligence by which he suffers nervous shock such as seeing his house on fire: *Attia v British Gas plc 1987*.

A person suffering nervous shock may have a claim if they can show that there was a sufficiently close relationship between themselves and the primary victim and that they either saw the accident with their unaided senses or came upon the 'immediate aftermath'.

> *McLoughlin v O'Brien 1982*
> *The facts:* The claimant was called to the hospital where her husband and children were receiving emergency treatment shortly after an accident caused by the defendant. She was informed that her daughter had died. She suffered nervous shock.

Decision: it was reasonably foreseeable that the claimant would be affected. She had a close relationship with the primary victims and came upon the immediate aftermath. Therefore she could recover damages.

It appears then that a distinction can be drawn between those who have a close family tie to the victim and a mere bystander. There is also a distinction between those who witness an event and are proximate to the accident in terms of time and space and those who are told of the accident or witness it via simultaneous television broadcast.

Alcock & Others v Chief Constable of South Yorkshire Police 1991

The facts: This case involves the Hillsborough disaster when 95 people were killed and another 400 injured due to being crushed in crowded stands. Various relatives of the victims, who had proved various psychiatric illnesses as a result of learning of the tragedy, being at the ground or witnessing it on television, brought an action against the defendants in negligence.

Decision: the claimants' claim must fail either because they could not establish a sufficient degree of kinship to make it reasonably foreseeable that psychiatric illness would result, or because they witnessed the accident via simultaneous (or recorded) broadcasts and therefore were not sufficiently proximate in time and space.

Vernon v Bosley 1997

Facts: Two young children were passengers in a car driven by the defendant, their nanny, when it went off the road and crashed into the river. The claimant, their father, did not see the accident but was called to the scene and witnessed the unsuccessful attempt to rescue the children. The claimant suffered nervous shock.

Decision: the claimant could recover damages from the defendant.

The Piper Alpha disaster in the North Sea produced further developments in this area. The issue was whether a duty of care was owed to a mere bystander who witnessed a horrific accident with his own unaided senses and subsequently suffered nervous shock.

McFarlane v E E Caledonia Ltd 1994

The facts: The claimant, an employee of the defendants, stood and witnessed the massive explosions on the oil rig in which 164 men were killed, before being evacuated by helicopter. As a result he suffered psychiatric illness and sued the defendants in negligence.

Decision: No duty of care was owed in these circumstances. The claimant had not been in fear for his own safety nor had he been in actual danger. He had no close relationship with the primary victims and had taken no active part in rescue operations. As a mere bystander he had no claim.

It is established then that a person who suffers nervous shock as a result of participating in the rescue of injured victims in an accident would be owed a duty of care.

Chadwick v British Railways Board 1967

The facts: A serious train crash occurred as a result of the negligence of the train driver. The claimant attended the scene and over a prolonged period of time helped in the rescue work. As a result he suffered nervous shock.

Decision: A duty of care was held to rescuers and as nervous shock was foreseeable in the circumstances. The defendants were liable.

Activity 4	**(5 mins)**

S and her daughter, A, visit the local fair owned by C. A has a ride on the big wheel. S watches in horror as the carriage in which A is riding becomes disconnected due to rust and decay and plummets to the ground. S suffers nervous shock. Consider whether S could sue C in negligence.

2 BREACH OF DUTY OF CARE

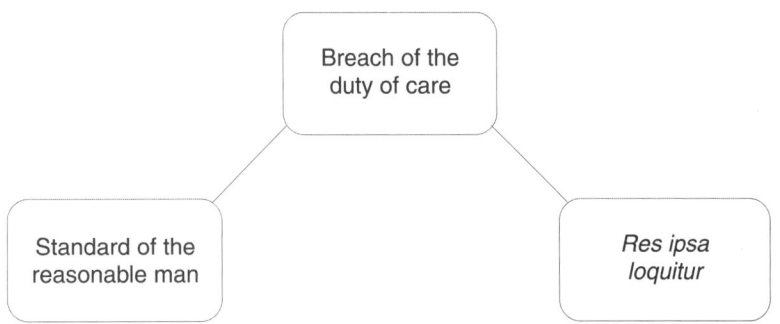

The standard of reasonable care requires that the person concerned should do what a reasonable man 'guided upon those considerations which ordinarily regulate the conduct of human affairs' would do and abstain from doing what a reasonable man would not do.

2.1 The standard of the 'reasonable man

'The standard of 'a reasonable man' is not that of an average man: for instance, the standard of a 'reasonable' car driver is a very high standard indeed, and would not be lowered for a learner driver. The rule has been developed as follows.

(a) In considering what precautions should be taken or foresight applied, the test is one of **knowledge and general practice existing at the time**, not hindsight or subsequent change of practice.

Roe v Minister of Health 1954
The facts: A doctor gave a patient an injection, taking all the precautions required at that time. The drug was contaminated and the patient became paralysed. At the time of the trial seven years later medical practice had been improved to avoid the risk of undetected contamination (through an invisible crack in a glass tube).

Decision: the proper test was normal practice based on the state of medical knowledge at the time. The doctor was not at fault in failing to anticipate later developments.

(b) A person who professes to have a **particular skill**, for example in a profession, is required to use the skill which he purports to have. But an error of judgement is not automatically a case of negligence: *Whitehouse v Jordan 1981*.

(c) In deciding what is reasonable care **the balance must be struck between advantage and risk**. The driver of a fire engine may exceed the normal prudent speed on his way to a fire but not on the way back.

    (d)   If A owes a duty of care to B and A knows that B is unusually **vulnerable**, a higher standard of care is expected. For example, B might be a child, an inexperienced employee given risky work to do or a person with a thin skull.

Paris v Stepney Borough Council 1951
The facts: P was employed by K on vehicle maintenance. P had already lost the sight of one eye. He was hammering metal. It was not the normal practice to issue protective goggles to men employed on this work since the risk of eye injury was small. A chip of metal flew into P's eye and blinded him.

Decision: although industrial practice did not require the use of goggles by workers with normal sight, a higher standard of care was owed to P because an injury to his remaining good eye would blind him. S had failed to maintain a proper standard of care in relation to P.

Activity 5   **(10 mins)**

An accountant advises a client to use a well known tax avoidance scheme. At the time when he does so, the Inland Revenue is challenging the scheme in the courts. In a test case, the High Court has found in favour of the Inland Revenue but the Court of Appeal has found in favour of the taxpayer, and an Inland Revenue appeal to the House of Lords is pending. If the Inland Revenue succeed, any taxpayer who has used the scheme will be substantially worse off than if he had not used the scheme. If the Inland Revenue were to succeed in the House of Lords and the client were to sue the accountant, would the accountant be able to rely on Roe v Minister of Health 1954 in his defence?

2.2   Res ipsa loquitur

It rests on the claimant to show both that the defendant owed him a duty of reasonable care and that the defendant failed in that duty. If the claimant does not know how the accident happened it may be difficult to demonstrate that it resulted from failure to take proper care. In some circumstances the claimant may argue that the facts speak for themselves (*res ipsa loquitur*): that want of care is the only possible explanation for what happened and negligence on the part of the defendant must be presumed.

To rely on this principle the claimant must first show that the thing which caused the injury was under the management and control of the defendant and that the accident was such as would not occur if those in control used proper care.

Scott v London & St Katharine Docks Co 1865
The facts: S was passing in front of the defendant's warehouse. Six bags of sugar fell on him.

Decision: in the absence of explanation it must be presumed that the fall of the bags of sugar was due to want of care on the part of the defendants.

Similarly, in *Mahon v Osborne 1939* the principle of *res ipsa loquitor* was agued when a surgeon left a swab inside a patient after an operation.

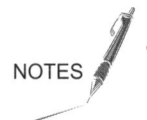

Activity 6   **(10 mins)**

E left her horse in a paddock surrounded by a high fence and with only one gate, but the horse got out of the paddock and injured J. E claims that she had shut the gate securely, but J claims that she had not disturbed the gate. It is certain that no other person was involved. What principle of the law of negligence might J try to rely on in suing E?

---

3 CONSEQUENTIAL HARM

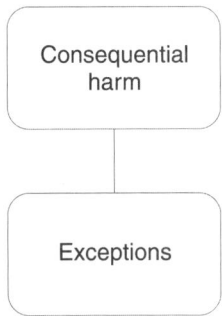

A claim for compensation for negligence will not succeed if damage or loss is not proved. In deciding whether a claim should be allowed, the court considers whether the breach of duty gave rise to the harm and whether the harm was too remote from the breach.

A person will only be compensated if he has suffered actual loss, injury, damage or harm as a consequence of another's actions.

3.1 Exceptions

The claim will not be proved if:

    (a)   the claimant followed a course of action regardless of the acts of the defendant;

    (b)   a third party is the actual cause of harm;

    (c)   a complicated series of events takes place such that no one act was the cause of all the harm; or

    (d)   an intervening act by the claimant or a third party breaks the chain of causation (*novus actus interveniens*).

Having decided whether harm arose from a breach of duty, the court will finally look at whether the harm which occurred was reasonably foreseeable. The legal issues were discussed in the previous chapter.

NOTES

4 NEGLIGENT MIS-STATEMENT

4.1 Professional advice

This section seeks to demonstrate how the law relating to negligent professional advice, and in particular **auditors**, has been developed through the operation of precedent, being refined and explained with each successive case that comes to court. It illustrates the often step-by-step development of English law, which has gradually refined the principles laid down in *Donoghue v Stevenson* and *Anns* to cover **negligent misstatements** which cause financial loss.

Before 1963, it was held that any liability for careless statements was limited in scope and depended upon the existence of a **contractual** or **fiduciary relationship** between the parties. Lord Denning's tests of a further (later termed 'special') relationship were laid down in the Court of Appeal in his dissenting judgement on *Candler v Crane, Christmas & Co 1951*.

Definition

> According to Lord Denning, to establish a **special relationship** the person who made the statement must have done so in some professional or expert capacity which made it likely that others would rely on what he said. This is the position of an adviser such as an accountant, banker, solicitor or surveyor.

It follows that a duty could not be owed to complete strangers, but Lord Denning also stated at the time: 'Accountants owe a duty of care not only to their own clients, but also to **all those whom they know will rely on their accounts** in the transactions for which those accounts are prepared.' This was to prove a significant consideration in later cases.

However, Lord Denning's view was a dissenting voice in 1951 in the *Candler* case, where the Court of Appeal held that the defendants were not liable (for a bad investment based upon a set of negligently prepared accounts) because there was no direct contractual or fiduciary relationship with the claimant investor.

It was twelve years later that the **special relationship** was accepted as a valid test. Our starting point is the **leading case** on negligent misstatement, outlined below, which was the start of a **new judicial approach** to cases involving negligent misstatement. You must make sure that you are familiar with it.

Hedley Byrne & Co Ltd v Heller and Partners Ltd 1963
The facts: HB were advertising agents acting for a new client, Easipower Ltd. HB requested information from Easipower's bank (HP) on its financial position. HP returned non-committal replies, which expressly disclaimed legal responsibility, and which were held to be negligent misstatement of Easipower's financial resources.

Decision: While HP were able to avoid liability by virtue of their disclaimer, the House of Lords went on to consider whether there ever could be a duty of care to avoid causing financial loss by negligent misstatement where there was no contractual or fiduciary relationship. It decided (as *obiter dicta*) that HP were guilty of negligence having breached the duty of care, because a special relationship did exist. Had it not been for the disclaimer, a claim for negligence would have succeeded.

In reaching the decision in *Hedley Byrne*, Lord Morris said the following:

> 'If someone possessed of a special skill undertakes....to apply that skill for the assistance of another person who **relies** on that skill, a duty of care will arise....If, in a sphere in which a person is so placed that others could reasonably rely on his skill....a person takes it on himself to give information or advice to....another person who, as he **knows or should know**, will place reliance on it, then a duty of care will arise.'

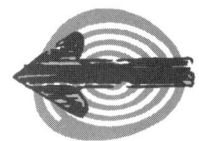

As you already know from your reading of Chapter 2, Section 2.2, obiter dicta such as those made in 1963 do not form part of the ratio decidendi, and are not binding on future cases. They will, however, be persuasive.

Note that at the time liability did not extend to those who the advisor might merely **foresee as a possible user** of the statement.

However in a subsequent case, the courts extended potential liability, and started to take account of third parties not known to the adviser. The following case echoed the principles laid down in *Anns* (Section 1.2) and addressed the question of **reasonable foresight** being present to create a duty of care.

JEB Fasteners Ltd v Marks, Bloom & Co 1982
The facts: The defendants, a firm of accountants, prepared an audited set of accounts showing overvalued stock and hence inflated profit. The auditors knew there were liquidity problems and that the company was seeking outside finance. The claimants were shown the accounts; they took over the company for a nominal amount, since by that means they could obtain the services of the company's two directors. At no time did MB tell JEB that the stock value was inflated. With the investment's failure, JEB sued MB, with the following claims.

(a) The accounts had been prepared negligently.

(b) They had relied on those accounts.

(c) They would not have invested had they been aware of the company's true position.

(d) MB owed a duty of care to **all persons whom they could reasonably foresee** would rely on the accounts.

Decision: Even though JEB had relied on the accounts (b), they would not have acted differently if the true position had been known (c), since they had really wanted the directors and not the company. Hence the accountants were not the cause of the consequential harm and were not liable. Significantly (although this did not affect the decision as to liability) it was the judge's view that MB did indeed owe a **duty of care through foresight** (d) and had been negligent in preparing the accounts (a).

Decisions since *JEB Fasteners* have, however, shied away from the foresight test and gone back to looking at whether the adviser has **knowledge of the user** and the **use to which the statement will be put**.

4.2 The Caparo decision

The Caparo case is fundamental to an understanding of this area.

This important and controversial case made considerable changes to the tort of negligence as a whole, and the negligence of professionals in particular, and set a precedent which now forms the basis for courts when considering the liability of professional advisers.

Caparo Industries plc v Dickman and Others 1990

The facts: Caparo, which already held shares in Fidelity plc, bought more shares and later made a takeover bid, after seeing accounts prepared by the defendants that showed a profit of £1.3m. Caparo claimed against the directors (the brothers Dickman) and the auditors for the fact that the accounts should have shown a loss of £400,000. The claimants argued that the auditors owed a duty of care to investors and potential investors in respect of the audit. They should have been aware that a press release stating that profits would fall significantly had made Fidelity vulnerable to a takeover bid and that bidders might well rely upon the accounts.

Decision: The auditor's duty did not extend to potential investors nor to existing shareholders increasing their stakes. It was a duty owed to the body of shareholders as whole.

In the *Caparo* case the House of Lords decided that there were two very different situations facing a person giving professional advice.

(a) Preparing information in the knowledge that a **particular person** was contemplating a transaction and would rely on the information in deciding whether or not to proceed with the transaction (the 'special relationship').

(b) Preparing a statement for **general circulation**, which could forseeably be relied upon by persons unknown to the professional for a variety of different purposes.

It was held therefore that a public company's auditors owed **no duty of care to the public at large** who relied on the audit report in deciding to invest - and, in purchasing additional shares, an existing shareholder was in no different position to the public at large.

In *MacNaughton (James) Papers Group Ltd v Hicks Anderson & Co 1991*, it was stated that it was necessary to examine each case in the light of the following.

- Foreseeability
- Proximity
- Fairness

This is because there could be **no single overriding principle** that could be applied to the individual complexities of every case. Lord Justice Neill set out the matters to be taken into account in considering this.

- The purpose for which the statement was **made**
- The purpose for which the statement was **communicated**
- The **relationship** between the maker of the statement, the recipient and any relevant third party
- The **size** of any class to which the recipient belonged
- The **state of knowledge** of the maker
- Any **reliance** by the recipient

The duty of care of accountants is held to be higher when advising on takeovers than when auditing. The directors and financial advisors of the target company in a contested takeover bid were held to owe a duty of care to a **known** take-over bidder in respect of financial statements prepared for the purpose of contesting the bid: *Morgan Crucible Co plc v Hill Samuel Bank Ltd and others 1990*.

A more recent case highlighted the need for a cautious approach and careful evaluation of the circumstances when giving financial advice, possibly with the need to issue a disclaimer.

> *ADT Ltd v BDO Binder Hamlyn 1995*
> *The facts:* Binder Hamlyn was the joint auditor of BSG. In October 1989, BSG's audited accounts for the year to 30 June 1989 were published. Binder Hamlyn signed off the audit as showing a true and fair view of BSG's position. ADT was thinking of buying BSG and, as a potential buyer, sought Binder Hamlyn's confirmation of the audited results. On 5 January 1990, the Binder Hamlyn audit partner attended a meeting with John Jermine, a director of ADT. This meeting was described by the judge as the 'final hurdle' before ADT finalised its bid for BSG. At the meeting, Mr Bishop specifically confirmed that he 'stood by' the audit of October 1989. ADT proceeded to purchase BSG for £105m. It was subsequently alleged that BSG's true value was only £40m. ADT therefore sued Binder Hamlyn for the difference, £65m plus interest.

> *Decision:* Binder Hamlyn assumed a responsibility for the statement that the audited accounts showed a true and fair view of BSG which ADT relied on to its detriment. Since the underlying audit work had been carried out negligently, Binder Hamlyn was held liable for £65m. The courts expect a higher standard of care from accountants when giving advice on company acquisitions since the losses can be so much greater.

This situation was different from *Caparo* since the court was specifically concerned with the **purpose of the statement made at the meeting**. Did Binder Hamlyn **assume any responsibility** as a result of Mr Bishop's comments? The court decided that it did. The

court did not need to consider the question of duty to individual shareholders, because *Caparo* had already decided that there was none.

Following the *ADT* case, another case tested the court's interpretation.

> *NRG v Bacon and Woodrow and Ernst & Young 1996*
> *The facts:* NRG alleged that the defendants had failed to suggest the possibility that certain companies it was targeting might suffer huge reinsurance losses. They had also failed to assess properly whether these losses could be protected against, because defective actuarial methods had been used. As a result, it overpaid for these companies by £255m.

> *Decision:* The judge observed that accountants owe a higher standard of care when advising on company purchases, because the potential losses are so much greater, following *ADT*. However, applying this higher standard of care to the facts, it was decided that NRG had received the advice that any competent professional would have given, because the complex nature of the losses that the companies were exposed to were not fully understood at the time. In addition, the use of defective actuarial methods had not led directly to the losses, because NRG would have bought the companies anyway.

There have been some other important clarifications of the law affecting accountants' liability in the area of responsibility towards non-clients. The following two cases both concerned auditors' liability to part of a group for losses incurred elsewhere in the group.

> *Barings plc v Coopers & Lybrand 1997*
> *The facts:* Barings collapsed in 1995 after loss-making trading by the general manager of its Singapore subsidiary, BFS. BFS was audited by the defendant's Singapore firm, which provided Barings directors with consolidation schedules and a copy of the BFS audit report. The defendant tried to argue that there was no duty of care owed to Barings, only to BFS.

> *Decision:* A duty of care was owed to Barings, as the defendants must have known that their audit report and consolidation schedules would be relied upon at group level.

> *BCCI (Overseas) Ltd v Ernst & Whinney 1997*
> *The facts:* In this case, the defendants audited the group holding company's accounts, but not those of the claimant subsidiary. The claimant tried to claim that the defendants had a duty of care to them.

> *Decision:* No duty of care was owed to the subsidiary because no specific information is normally channelled down by a holding company's auditor to its subsidiaries.

UK accountancy firms have been investigating ways of limiting liability in the face of increasing litigation. KPMG, for example, incorporated its audit practice as early as 1995.

In 2000, the Limited Liability Partnerships Act 2000 was passed, and limited liability partnerships have been permitted under law since 2001. Many firms of accountants have now adopted limited liability status.

Activity 7 (10 mins)

At a party, A asks B, a friend of his and a solicitor, about a dispute which he is having with his neighbour. B suggests that A comes to her office for a chat about it the next day. He does so, and B gives him some advice without charge. He acts upon that advice, and in consequence loses his right to sue his neighbour. Discuss whether A could sue B.

Activity 8 (10 mins)

An electrical engineer writes a book for general publication on the safe use of electricity. The advice given is generally sound, but there are certain circumstances in which precautions not mentioned in the book should be taken. Consider whether someone who suffers injury through not taking these precautions could sue the author in negligence.

Chapter roundup

- Negligence is causing loss by failing to take reasonable care when there is a duty to do so. A duty of care is owed to persons whom it could be reasonably be foreseen would be affected by the defendant's carelessness.

- The claimant may be expected to have taken reasonable and expected precautions, and defendants are not liable for the actions of third parties not under their control.

- Liability for economic loss is limited to cases in which there is a special relationship between the claimant and the defendant.

- Nervous shock is not generally actionable except by persons in fear of their own safety, witnesses actually present and relatives who learn of an accident immediately afterwards.

- The standard of reasonable care varies with the expertise of the defendant and with the circumstances, but later improvements in methods are not taken into account.

- Where there is no explanation for how an accident happened but want of care is the only possible explanation, the doctrine of res ipsa loquitur may be invoked.

- Damages are only recoverable for the consequences of the defendant's actions. The actions of third parties, or the actions of the claimant uninfluenced by the defendant's actions, may break the chain of causation and prevent damages from being awarded.

- Negligent misstatements by experts are actionable, but there is uncertainty about how widely a duty of care is owed. The most important recent case is *Caparo Industries plc v Dickman and Others 1990*.

Quick quiz

1 What is required to establish a valid claim for negligence?

2 How far has liability for want of care been restricted by developments in case law?

3 To what extent are damages recoverable for nervous shock.

4 Explain the significance of *res ipsa loquitur*.

5 How is a special relationship established in a case of negligent professional advice?

Answers to quick quiz

1 Duty of care
Breach of the duty
Resultant loss (see introduction)

2 There must be a sufficient relationship of proximity.
Defendant should be able to foresee that carelessness may cause harm.
Law recognises that the duty results in liability.

3 A definite and identifiable psychiatric illness must have been suffered by the defendant.

4 It enables the claimant to avoid having to prove that the defendant was in breach of the duty of care.

5 Person acts in a professional or expert capacity.
Likely that others will rely on what he says.
Must foresee that it is likely to be relied upon.

Answers to activities

1 D. The elements in options 1, 2 and 4 are the formulation of the tort of negligence as in *Anns* and *Caparo*. If these are present then there is a right of action for the tort of negligence.

2 It is for public policy reasons that barristers may not be sued in negligence. If every unsuccessful litigant sued his barrister this would effectively lead to a retrial and excessive litigation which would be detrimental to the legal system and justice.

3 No: A is not responsible for the actions of third parties and he has no duty of care or responsibility to B.

4 S could claim damages for nervous shock because she witnessed the accident with her own unaided senses and has a sufficiently close relationship (mother and child) with the primary victim, A.

5 No: the accountant knew (or at least should have known) of the risk.

6 J could sue E for negligence and rely on the principle of *res ipsa loquitur*. The horse was under the control and management of E and the facts speak for themselves.

7 A could sue B for negligent misstatement because B is giving advice in the capacity of solicitor (rather than friend) in a formal business context.

8 An action for negligent misstatement in these circumstances would fail due to the absence of a special relationship between the author and injured party.

Assignment 7 (30 mins)

(a) Explain the expression 'standard of care' in the tort of negligence.

(b) Flash, a financial journalist, is attending a business promotion where he meets Dale, a fashion model. Over a glass of champagne, he advises her to buy shares in Ming Ltd. Dale follows his advice.

Zarkov overhears the conversation between Flash and Dale at the promotion and he too decides to buy shares in Ming Ltd, but before doing so he first checked the last report of the auditors of Ming's accounts. The report was of a positive nature.

The price of Ming's shares has now fallen sharply and is unlikely to recover.

Advise Dale and Zarkov on whether they have any claim in tort for their losses.

ANSWERS TO ASSIGNMENTS

Answer to assignment 1 (Chapter 4)

(a) **Advertisement**. In the law of contract an **offer** is a definite promise to another to be bound on specific terms. Only an offer made with the intention that it shall become binding when accepted may be converted into a contract by acceptance. An offer can be made to a particular person or persons or to the public at large. An **invitation to treat**, by contrast, is an indication that someone is **prepared to receive offers** with the view to forming a binding contract. An invitation to treat is not capable of being accepted so as to form a legally binding contract.

Case law has established a number of accepted principles which apply to determine whether something is an offer or merely an invitation to treat. As a general rule, an **advertisement** is not of itself an offer capable of acceptance but is usually regarded as an attempt to induce offers and therefore is an invitation to treat (*Partridge v Crittenden*). Similarly, the circulation of a price list also constitutes an invitation to treat. In limited circumstances, an advertisement may constitute an offer as in *Carlill v Carbolic Smoke Ball Co*, where the words of the advertisement were very clear and precise and were held to be an offer to the world at large, capable of being accepted by anyone fulfilling the necessary conditions.

Adam's advertisement may be regarded as an offer rather than an invitation to treat, owing to the very clear and categorical language used (following Carlill's case). His advertisement is 'a serious offer', clearly stating the price and open to acceptance by the first person to respond.

(b) There is a general rule in the law of contract that **acceptance** must be express (oral or written) or implied and must be **communicated** to the offeror before it can be effective, unless the offeror expressly waives the need for communication (Carlill's case). The offeror may stipulate the exact means of communication in which case only compliance with his or her terms will suffice.

The **postal rule** provides an exception to this. The postal rule provides that where the use of the post is in the contemplation of both parties and the acceptance is correctly put in the post, then acceptance will be valid once posted, whether or not the offeror actually receives the letter: *Adams v Lindsell*. Whether the use of post was in the contemplation of the parties may be deduced from the circumstances, for example if the offer was itself made by post (*Household Fire and Carriage Accident Insurance Co v Grant*).

In this case it is clearly not appropriate for acceptance to be made by post. The offer is valid for one day only and the car will be sold to the 'first person who accepts it'. It is implicit that a more immediate communication of acceptance was required. Ben has not entered into a binding contract with Adam.

(c) Acceptance must be **unqualified agreement** to the terms of the offer. Where the 'acceptance' actually introduces some new term it constitutes a **counter-offer**. A counter-offer operates to reject the original offer and is itself open to acceptance or rejection by the original offeror (*Hyde v Wrench*).

In purporting to accept Adam's offer contained in the advertisement, Carol is altering the terms by seeking to pay by cheque rather than cash. The offer clearly requires payment in cash. The decision in *D & C Builders v Rees* to the effect that payment by cheque is equal to payment by cash would not be applied in this case, where payment by cash and not by cheque is expressly intended and required. Carol has made a counter-offer that Adam is free to accept or reject.

(d) The offeror may revoke the offer, by communicating revocation to the offeree, at any time up to acceptance (*Payne v Cave*) unless by a separate option agreement, for which consideration has been given, he has agreed to keep the offer open for a certain period of time (*Routledge v Grant*). A simple promise, unsupported by consideration, to keep the offer open is not binding.

It appears that Dave provided no consideration in return for Adam's promise to keep the offer open and so no contract arose and Adam's promise was not binding. Dave could argue, however, that his entering into a loan with his bank constituted consideration. If successful, Adam would be in breach of contract if he refused to sell the car to Dave.

(e) Eric introduced a new term as to price and his counter offer is accepted by Adam. Thus a binding contract comes into existence and by refusing to pay for and accept the car, Eric is in breach of contract. Adam is entitled to sue Eric for the price. He might be better advised to sell the car to Dave for £5,000 and sue Eric for the remaining £1,000.

Answer to assignment 2 (Chapter 5)

Ann is seeking to rely on the separate agreement of each of the parties with whom she contracted to accept something other than the consideration originally agreed as satisfying the whole contractual debt.

The situations described raise three separate questions:

- Can payment in kind (here, a painting) constitute consideration?

- Can payment of a lesser sum by a third party constitute consideration?

- Can a party who has accepted a lesser amount be estopped from claiming the full amount?

Consideration

Consideration was defined in *Currie v Misa* as follows: 'A valuable consideration…may consist either in some right, interest, protection or benefit accruing to one party, or some forbearance, detriment, loss or responsibility given, suffered or undertaken by the other'.

Thus forbearance, or the waiver, of existing rights can amount to consideration. As in all cases, **one party's promise must be supported by consideration on the part of the other party**. Hence if a party to a contract agrees to waive his right to a part of a debt, it is clear under the general principles of contract law that this promise must itself be supported by consideration.

In *Foakes v Beer*, the defendant had obtained judgement against the plaintiff for a debt. By written agreement, the defendant agreed to accept payment by instalments of the sum due, with no mention being made of interest which was also due.

The plaintiff paid off the amount and the defendant then claimed the interest as well, arguing that her written agreement (promise) did not prevent her from claiming the interest as this promise was not supported by consideration. It was held that she was indeed entitled to the debt with interest, as the plaintiff had provided no consideration for any waiver of rights.

There are **situations**, however, **in which a waiver may be binding** even if the debtor apparently gives **no consideration** (known as exceptions to the rule in Pinnel's case), including the following:

(i) Where the debtor offers and the creditor accepts anything to which the creditor was not originally entitled, for example,

- Goods instead of cash
- Payment before the date on which settlement is due *(Pinnel's case)*

(ii) Where the debtor makes an arrangement with his creditors that they will each accept part payment in full settlement, the debtor can hold the creditors individually to the agreed terms

(iii) Where a **third party offers part payment** and the creditor agrees to waive his rights against the debtor, the creditor has received consideration from the third party against whom he had no previous claim *(Welby v Drake)*

(iv) Where the principle of **promissory estoppel** applies.

Promissory Estoppel

The principle of promissory estoppel is, if a creditor makes a promise which is not supported by consideration to the debtor that the creditor will release the debtor from some of the debt, the creditor intends the debtor to act on this and the debtor does so, then the creditor may be estopped from retracting his promise unless the debtor can be restored to his original position.

The principle was developed in the case of *Central London Property Trust v High Trees House*. In this landmark case, the plaintiffs had, in September 1939, let a block of flats to the defendants, agreeing an annual rent of £2,500 per annum. As it was difficult to let the flats during wartime, the plaintiffs agreed in January 1940, in writing, to accept a reduced rent of £1,250. No stipulation was made as to the duration of this arrangement, but it was clear that it related to wartime conditions.

The defendants paid the reduced rent from 1940 to 1945, subletting flats at rents set on the basis of their own expected liability to pay rent under the revised agreement with the plaintiffs. In 1945, when the flats were fully let, the plaintiffs demanded the original rent of £2,500 per annum for the final two quarters of 1945.

It was held that the agreement of January 1940 was a temporary expedient only and had ceased to apply in early 1945. The plaintiffs' claim was therefore upheld. However, in an important obiter dictum which forms the basis of the principle of promissory estoppel, Denning J (later Lord Denning) said that had the plaintiffs sued for the full rent in respect of the earlier periods, the 1940 agreement would have served to defeat the claim and they would not have been allowed to go back on their promise.

The **defendants had relied on the promise given**. The doctrine of promissory estoppel operates as a **shield only and not a sword**, that is, the defendants could not have sought to sue on the promise relying on the doctrine *(Combe v Combe)*. Promissory estoppel applies only to a waiver of rights that is **given voluntarily**. If the creditor agrees to waive existing rights reluctantly or under pressure the doctrine does not apply and he can later claim the full sum *(D and C Builders v Rees)*.

Application to Ann

Applying these principles to the facts of the three cases, the following conclusions can be drawn:

(a) **Belle**. As Belle accepts a painting in place of the £500 owed to her, she falls within one of the exceptions to the rule in Pinnel's case and cannot claim payment of the original debt.

(b) **Chas**. Chas also falls within one of the exceptions as he accepts a lesser sum from a third party as consideration for releasing his entitlement to the full sum as in *Welby v Drake*. He cannot, therefore, claim payment of the balance of £1,500.

(c) **Dan**. Dan's agreement to accept £3,000 rather than £5,000 must be supported by consideration on Ann's part to be enforceable and this does not appear to be the case. Applying *Foakes v Beer* he may claim the balance.

None of the exceptions to the rule apply given that his **agreement was given reluctantly** as in *D and C Builders v Rees*. This means that promissory estoppel does not apply.

Even if promissory estoppel did apply, Ann would need to argue not only that Dan promised to waive his entitlement to the full debt but also that she acted on his promise to her detriment. There is nothing to suggest that this is the case.

Answer to assignment 3 (Chapter 6)

A contract is a legally binding agreement. Hence a mere agreement is not a contract unless there is evidence, express or implied, of the intention of the parties that their agreement should give rise to legal relations or legally binding obligations.

Express statements

In making an agreement, the parties may expressly say that it is or it is not intended to create legal relations. In one leading case, a written agreement stated that 'this agreement is not entered into...as a formal or legal agreement': *Rose & Frank Co v J T Crompton and Bros Ltd 1925*.

As an example of the opposite case it is provided by statute that an agreement between an employer and a trade union on conditions of employment etc is not to be legally binding unless the parties state in writing that it shall be: s 179 Trade Union and Labour Relations (Consolidation) Act 1992.

Although an express statement of intention either way will always be accepted by the courts, it is not often possible to settle the matter in that way. The parties do not usually express any intention of this kind at all. In those circumstances the courts interpret the agreement which the parties have made by objective criteria, based on the words used, the subject-matter of the contract, the relationship of the parties and so on. In this way the courts seek to deduce what is the presumed but unexpressed intention of the parties.

Presumptions

In *commercial agreements*, the courts will normally infer that there is an intention to create legal relations unless there is evidence to the contrary. In *Edwards v Skyways 1964* an agreement entered into to make an 'ex-gratia' payment as part of a larger negotiation was held to be legally binding.

The issue may sometimes arise when a supplier of goods has published an advertisement which may be an offer to sell the goods or to give some guarantee in respect of them. In the well-known carbolic smoke ball case (*Carlill v Carbolic Smoke Ball Co 1893*) the manufacturer argued - unsuccessfully - that his offer to pay a sum of money to any user of his medicine (who was not protected by it) was a mere 'puff' not intended to create a legally binding agreement.

The court decided against him because his advertisement stated that as proof of the seriousness of his assurance he had deposited money in a bank account

to meet claims. This fact overrode any deduction about the general effect of an advertisement.

At one time, it was considered that in an agreement made in a *domestic context* there was no implied intention to create legal relations if none had been expressed. Thus an agreement by a husband to pay an allowance to his wife during his absence abroad was not legally binding: *Balfour v Balfour 1919*.

However, the courts are now more readily disposed to assume that there is an intention to create legal relations in an agreement between husband and wife, especially if they are no longer living together: *Merritt v Merritt 1969*. But much also depends on how the parties express their agreement. In *Merritt's* case, the wife insisted that the agreement be in writing so that the husband should sign it. In another case, a husband on leaving home promised to pay £15 per week to his wife 'so long as I can manage it'; this commitment was held to be so vague that no intention to create a legal obligation should be assumed: *Gould v Gould 1969*.

In other relationships, the court is more readily disposed to assume that the parties, although relatives or friends, did intend that a financial agreement should be binding. This may apply if there is a 'mutuality of agreement' amounting to a joint enterprise, for example where persons jointly enter a competition: *Simpkins v Pays 1955*. In this case, a woman, her granddaughter and a paying lodger took part in a weekly competition in a newspaper, which they entered in the grandmother's name. One week they won £750 and the lodger was denied a third share. It was held that there was a mutuality of agreement and that this was not a friendly adventure but a contract.

Answer to assignment 5 (Chapter 7)

There are two important clauses to consider in Brian's encounter with the car park. The first is 'closed circuit television in operation' and the second is 'cars parked at owners' risk. No responsibility ... etc ...'. The status of the first clause is unclear. It could amount to a representation, inducing the formation of the contract but not becoming a contract term, or it could be construed as a term of the contract. The remedies available to Brian will differ depending on the position. The second clause is a notice which purports to exclude liability and may therefore have the status at law of an exclusion clause, by which the car park operator will, as is seen in the conversation between Brian and the attendant, seek to exclude any liability on its part for Brian's loss.

Taking the two matters in reverse order, as this is the sequence in which they are considered when Brian seeks a remedy from the car park operator, the following matters require consideration in relation to the exclusion clause. As exclusion clauses are open to abuse by a stronger party where the persons making the contract are of unequal bargaining power, the law departs from its usual position of allowing parties to govern their own contractual relations and imposes some restrictions on their use. Certain types of clause are void by statute, while others will be examined by the courts firstly to ensure that they are properly incorporated into the contract and secondly to interpret the clause.

Only in limited circumstances will the courts allow the incorporation of a term after the contract has been made. It may only be done by the mutual agreement of the parties. Thus a sign on a hotel room wall was not incorporated into the contract between hotel and client since it was not seen until after the contract was made: *Olley v Marlborough Court 1949*. The court will have regard to the nature of the liability which is being excluded when deciding whether a clause has been effectively incorporated. If the terms are particularly unusual or wide, a more prominent notice may be necessary. For

example, in *Thornton v Shoe Lane Parking Ltd 1971* a notice excluding liability for injury in an automatic car park was not sufficiently displayed or referred to at the time the contract was made). The terms may be incorporated into the contract by the signature of the other party on a document bearing the terms. The signatory is taken to know of the terms, even if he could not read them: *L'Estrange v Graucob 1934*. Where the parties deal frequently in transactions of a similar nature and on the same terms, the courts are ready to hold that the exclusion clause has been incorporated into the latest agreement by virtue of its being present in the previous dealings. However, it is not enough that the other party ought to have known of the clause; he must actually be aware of it: *Hollier v Rambler Motors 1972*.

As well as controlling the incorporation of exclusion clauses into contracts, the courts have developed other restrictions on their use. They tend to interpret them strictly, in favour of the weaker party. This is the *contra preferentem* rule. They presume that the clause is not intended to defeat the main purpose of the contract. If the clause limits liability in general terms, the courts will construe its scope so as to give the party relying on it the minimum opportunity to escape liability. A general exemption will not usually be interpreted so as to cover negligence: *Hollier v Rambler Motors 1972*. Statute law also imposes some very important restrictions on the use of exclusion clauses. The Unfair Contract Terms Act 1977 divides these clauses into two types; those which are void and those which are valid only as far as they are reasonable. Liability for personal injury or death due to negligence may never be excluded. An exclusion for loss due to negligence in other circumstances will be valid only insofar as it is reasonable: s 2 UCTA 1977.

In standard term contracts made with a consumer, terms which seek to exclude liability for breach, or to allow substantially different performance, or no performance at all, are valid only insofar as they are reasonable: s 3. Reasonableness is to be considered with reference to the factors in s 11. The court will consider the relative strength of the parties' bargaining power, whether an inducement was offered to the consumer, whether the consumer knew or ought to have known of the exclusion clauses and whether compliance with the contract's terms so that the exclusion clause would never be needed was practicable (Sch 2).

The wording of the question makes it clear that there is a contract between Brian and Secure Car Parks Ltd (ie this is not a free car park). The first issue to consider is therefore whether the clause was incorporated into the contract or not. A notice of this type may be inadequate if not seen until after the contract was entered into: *Olley v Marlborough Court 1949*. However an analogy may be drawn with the printing of conditions on a railway ticket in *Thompson v LMS Railway 1930*. Here, the ticket was given at the time the contract was made and, if the notice was visible at the same time, it is likely that the notice is part of the contract. If the ticket contained reference to the notice, as in *Thompson v LMS Railway 1930*, the notice may still be binding on Brian (although this is more likely to be so if Brian had used the car park previously and so had constructive and/or actual notice of it, and this appears to be his first visit).

As noted earlier there is a well-known case which actually concerns a car park - *Thornton v Shoe Lane Parking Ltd 1972*. Here it was held that a contract was formed before the plaintiff received the car park ticket: the 'parking' sign was an offer and his act of parking was acceptance. A notice disclaiming liability for damage to cars which was on display inside the car park after the ticket was received was therefore found not to be validly included in the contract.

Here, Brian has not yet got his ticket, but he is in the process of parking when he sees the sign. The case is not clear-cut, but will probably depend on, for

example, whether or not he is able to turn his car round at this point. Assuming though that *Thornton* is followed, the act of parking may be held to be the critical point at which the contract is made and, since Brian is actually driving in to the car park and is about to take a ticket when he sees the sign, he therefore has notice of the clause before the contract is made. Secure Car Parks Ltd would therefore be able to rely on the clause.

As the term covers damage to property it must be decided whether it is reasonable within s 2 of the 1977 Act. This will depend on the criteria of Sch 2: the relative strength of the parties, the offer of inducements to enter into the contract, awareness of the effect of the contract and so on.

On being informed of the effect of the exclusion clause, Brian turns to the matter of the closed circuit television. Whether the sign is a representation or a contract term will depend on the following.

(a)   The interval of time between the statement being made and the contract coming into effect. The later the statement is made the more likely it is to be a term of the contract.

(b)   Whether the party making the statement is in a position of special knowledge. If he is, the statement is more likely to be a term of the contract.

In Brian's case, both these tests suggest that the statement is a contract term. Under normal circumstances, Brian would therefore have a claim against Secure Car Parks Ltd for breach of contract, and seek to claim damages against the company. However, if, as supposed above, the exclusion clause is a valid one, this may not be possible. Turning to s 3 of UCTA, this states that, in standard term contracts made with a consumer, terms which seek to exclude liability (of the person imposing the term) for breach, or to allow substantially different performance, or no performance at all, are valid only insofar as they are reasonable. The court will therefore have to consider further whether the exclusion clause is reasonable. The fact that there is an 'inducement' to enter the car park - in the form of the sign about closed circuit TV itself - may well count against the car park operator.

Answer to assignment 6 (Chapter 8)

(a)   (i)   It is important to be able to distinguish between an employee and an independent contractor for a number of reasons. For example, the distinction will enable the courts to determine the vicarious liability of the employer, who is vicariously liable only for the negligence of his employees, save in very exceptional circumstances. An **employee is someone employed by his or her employer under the terms of a formal contract of employment**. An **independent contractor** has been defined as ' **a self-employed person who contracts to provide services for another but does not enter into a contract of employment as an employee of that other'**. Sometimes the distinction between the two is very obvious - such as where there is a contract for services or where the employer deducts PAYE and NI from the worker's gross pay - but often it will not be obvious. A number of **tests** may be applied in order to distinguish between the two types of worker.

The **expressed intentions of the parties will not necessarily be conclusive** *(Ferguson v John Dawson & Partners 1976)*. The courts will apply three tests - of control, integration and economic reality.

The **control test** asks whether the employer has control over the way in which the employee performs his duties. In *Mersey Docks & Harbour*

Board v Coggins & Griffiths (Liverpool) Ltd 1947, a driver of a crane could be instructed by the employer what to do but not how to do his work and it was held that he was an independent contractor since *(inter alia)* the 'employer' lacked sufficient control properly to be called an employer. In some circumstances, it is not possible to establish whether a person is an employee by reference to a single test, but the control test is often thought to provide a reasonably authoritative guide.

The **integration test** applies where the employee has such a degree of skill that he cannot be 'controlled' in the performance of his duties and asks whether he was appointed and assigned to his duties by the employer, ie did he become an integral part of the employer's business organisation or did his work remain outside of and merely accessory to it? Thus in *Cassidy v Ministry of Health 1951*, it was held that a skilled surgeon was the employee of the Ministry of Health since, although the Ministry could not possibly control the doctor in his medical work, it (and not the patient) had selected him and integrated him into the organisation.

The **economic reality or 'multiple' test** asks whether the employee is working on his own account. Here the court will consider all relevant factors including the employer's right to appoint and dismiss, the basis on which payment is made, whether tax and NI is deducted, who provides the tools and equipment, the number of 'employers': *RMC (SE) v Ministry of Pensions and NI 1968*. The courts will also consider whether the employee is entitled to delegate all his obligations (in which case there is no contract of employment), whether he is restricted in his place of work, obliged to work and whether holidays and hours of work are agreed: *O'Kelly v Trusthouse Forte plc 1983*.

(ii) **The second prerequisite of vicarious liability is that the employee was acting in the course of his employment**. Broadly, this means that he must have been carrying on work for which he was employed.

The employer will be liable for any act which he expressly authorised, even if the act was only tortious because it was wrongfully performed. Moreover, there may be vicarious liability even for an act which the employer expressly forbade, provided that it was done in the scope of the employment or in furtherance of the employer's business *(Limpus v London General Omnibus Co 1862)*. This case involved a bus driver who caused an accident even though he had been forbidden from obstructing buses of rival firms. In *Beard v London General Omnibus Co 1900*, a conductor was forbidden to drive buses. He caused an accident while driving a bus. Here, the employer was not liable, as his instructions served to demarcate the limits of the conductor's job. When the accident occurred, he was not doing the job for which he had been employed.

If an employee does something for his own convenience while carrying out his duties and this act is negligent, the employer may still be liable. For example, a driver of a petrol tanker who threw away a lighted match while making a delivery caused an explosion. His employer was liable, as the driver was acting in the course of his employment: *Century Insurance v Northern Ireland Road Transport Board 1942*. By comparison, in *Warren v Henlys 1948*, a petrol pump attendant became involved in an argument with a customer and struck him. The employer was not liable, since the assault was not within the course of the attendant's employment. The court found that this was a

personal act of the employee following the act of selling petrol, rather than something that happened in the course of the sale.

There have been many cases involving the use of vehicles. In *Twine v Bean's Express 1946*, a notice in the driver's cab in a van expressly forbade drivers from giving lifts. A passenger was taken on board and was killed in an ensuing accident. It was held that he was a trespasser and that the driver was not acting in the course of his employment in offering a lift to him. By comparison, in *Rose v Plenty 1976*, the driver of a milk float took a 13 year old boy on his milk round and the boy helped with the deliveries. The boy was injured and the court found that the employee was acting in the course of his employment, even though the driver had disobeyed orders, probably because the boy was helping with the deliveries of milk.

If the employee, acting in the course of his employment, defrauds a third party for his own advantage, the employer may still be vicariously liable: *Lloyd v Grace Smith & Co 1912.*

(b) Under the Occupiers' Liability Act 1957, **an occupier of premises owes a 'common duty of care' to all visitors to those premises**. An occupier of premises is the person who has control of the premises. He must take such precautions as are necessary to make those premises reasonably safe for the purposes for which the visitor has entered them. **The standard of care may vary with the visitor**. For example, specialists called on to the premises to deal with a hazard might be expected to be aware of the extra incidental risks (*Roles v Nathan 1963*) whereas a higher than usual standard is expected where the visitor is a child. Warnings which are deemed adequate for adults may not be adequate for children, as children may not read warnings and may be particularly attracted to risky ventures.

The common duty of care is owed to lawful visitors. A visitor is a person who has entered the premises either by virtue of a legal right of entry or at the express or implied invitation of the occupier. A person entering premises to do business with an occupier is deemed to have permission to enter, even if the occupier does not wish to see that visitor, for example a sales representative.

The occupier can discharge his duty by taking all reasonable steps to remove hazards or by giving due warnings of hazards where warnings are sufficient to enable the visitor to be reasonably safe (and a warning will not always be considered sufficient). If the visitor disregards the warning he may be taken to have consented to the risk or be guilty of contributory negligence.

If the visitor exceeds the limits of the permission (for example if he enters parts of the premises unconnected with the purpose of his visit), **he becomes a trespasser**. Under the Occupiers' Liability Act 1984, **the occupier owes a duty to trespassers if**

(i) **He is aware of the danger** or has reasonable grounds to believe that it exists,

(ii) **He knows or should know that someone is in** (or may come into) **the vicinity of the danger** and

(iii) **The risk is one against which he may reasonably be expected to offer that person some protection**.

'Trespasser' is not defined by the Act but, generally speaking, it is a person who knows he does not intend communication with the occupier or anyone else on the premises (*BR v Herrington 1972*). The duty owed is to take such care as is reasonable in all the circumstances to see that the person to whom a duty is owed does not suffer injury on the premises by reason of the danger. It can be discharged by taking reasonable steps to give warning of the danger. In the case of trespassers, the occupier can only be liable for personal injury and not damage to property.

In this case, Russell is a trespasser since he intends no communication with the occupier or anyone else on the premises. Provided that Usha can be regarded as the occupier of the premises, Usha owes him a duty to take such care as is reasonable in all the circumstances to see that he does no suffer injury on the premises by reason of the danger. **In the absence of any warnings about the rusty barbed wire fence, Usha faces potential liability for the personal injury suffered by Russell but not for the damage to his jacket. If Russell is a child, then even a warning would be likely to be considered inadequate to discharge the duty owed**.

Kylie is a lawful visitor since she has a legal right of entry. Usha owes her a duty to take such precautions as are necessary to make the premises reasonably safe for her purposes. She could discharge this duty by giving appropriate warnings, supplying hard hats and similar measures. **If she has failed to take any such steps she may be liable for the injury suffered by Kylie**. Any general notice which purports to exclude liability for death or personal injury resulting from negligence will be void (UCTA 1977).

Answer to assignment 7 (Chapter 9)

(a) The claimant must show that there has been a breach of the duty of care, that is, that the defendant has failed to meet the necessary standard of care, such as would be met by a reasonable man 'guided upon those considerations which ordinarily regulate the conduct of human affairs'. The standard is that for a reasonable man, not an average man. Several principles have been developed by the courts in considering the level of care which can be expected.

Hindsight or subsequent change of practice should not be relevant in considering what precautions should be taken or foresight applied. In *Roe v Minister of Health*, a patient became paralysed following an injection where the doctor took the normal precautions known at the time. The trial was held seven years later by which time medical practice had improved to include precautions which might have detected the contamination. It was held that the proper test was normal practice based on medical knowledge at the time of the injection. An error of judgment by a professional will not automatically be negligence although if a person professes to have a particular skill, he is required to display that skill: *Whitehouse v Jordan 1981*. If the person to whom the duty of care is owed is particularly vulnerable for some reason, and that is known to the person

owing the duty of care, a higher standard of care will be expected: *Paris v Stepney BC 1951*.

(b) **There is a duty of care not to cause financial loss by negligent misstatement**. This duty arises where the person making the statement foresees that it may be relied on, that is, where there is a **'special relationship'** between the parties. To establish a special relationship, the person making the statement must:

(i) Do so in some **professional or expert capacity** which makes it likely that others will rely on what he says, and

(ii) **Must foresee that it is likely to be relied on** by another person.

A financial adviser providing advice usually does so in a professional or expert capacity and the principle can also be extended by the courts to cover a situation where advice is given against a business background: *Chaudrey v Prabhakar 1989*. In *Hedley Byrne v Heller 1964*, advertising agents acting for a new client were given misleading advice about the client by the client's bank. The agents were able to establish that a special relationship existed between them and the bank and hence that they were owed a duty of care. The bank was held to be negligent and only escaped liability because of a valid disclaimer. In this case, the House of Lords adopted Lord Denning's test of a special relationship, as laid down in *Candler v Crane Christmas 1951*: 'a special relationship is one where the defendant gives advice or information and the plaintiff relies on that advice. The defendant should realise that his words will be relied on either by the person he is addressing or by a third party'. In contrast, it is unlikely that advice given on a social occasion would give rise to a duty of care, unless the person giving it realised (or should have realised) that it was going to be relied on.

Dale will have to demonstrate that the **'business promotion'** which she attends is more in the **nature of a business event rather than a social event** if she is to succeed in a claim against Flash. This will be difficult given for example the fact that champagne is available. Furthermore **it is not clear that Dale is in any way officially connected with the event and, as a journalist, he may be no more of an expert than Dale herself.**

As regards Zarkhov, he too is unlikely to have any claim against Flash for the same reasons and the fact that Flash did not make the statement to him, he simply overheard it. However, he should also consider whether or not a case against Ming's auditors could succeed.

The case of *Caparo Industries plc v Dickman 1990* summarises the current law on negligent professional advice. In this case, the House of Lords identified two different situations facing a person giving professional advice:

(i) The preparation of advice or information in the knowledge that a particular person is contemplating a transaction and is expecting to receive the advice or information in order to rely on it to decide whether or not to proceed with the transaction.

(ii) The preparation of a statement (for example an audit report) for more or less general circulation and which can foreseeably be relied

on by persons unknown to the auditor for a variety of different purposes.

Only the first of these circumstances involves a special relationship. As a result, the auditors of a public company owe no duty of care to the public at large who may rely on the audit report on deciding to invest. In the *Caparo* case, the action against the auditors was brought by an existing shareholder who had made an additional investment and this shareholder was held to be in a position no different from the public at large.

An example of a special relationship, in spite of the wide application of the *Caparo* case, can be seen in *Morgan Crucible Co plc v Hill Samuel Bank Ltd 1990*. In this case, the directors and financial advisers of the target company had made express representations to a known bidder, intending that the bidder should rely on those representations. It was held that they owed the bidder a duty of care not to be negligent in making representations which might mislead him.

In the *Caparo* case, described above, the court held that the auditors' duty did not extend to potential investors nor to existing shareholders increasing their stakes. It was a duty owed to the body of shareholders as a whole. However, the House of Lords did state that the necessary proximity could arise where auditors had prepared advice or information in the knowledge that a particular person was contemplating a transaction and was expecting to receive the advice or information in order to rely on it in making a decision whether or not to proceed with the transaction. There is nothing to suggest that such was the case here.

Ming's auditors therefore owed no duty of care to Zarkhov when they gave their audit report, as there was no special relationship between the parties.

GLOSSARY OF BUSINESS LAW TERMS

Acceptance An unqualified agreement to the terms of the offer.

Anticipatory breach Renunciation by party to a contract of his contractual obligations before the date for performance.

Arbitration A means of settling a dispute outside the courts.

Bill of exchange A type of order to pay money.

Capacity The ability or power of a person to enter into legal relationships or carry out legal acts.

Claimant The person who complains or brings an action asking the court for relief (used to be called the plaintiff)

Code of practice A code which lays out a set of procedures and policies that a firm will follow.

Common law The body of legal rules developed by the common law courts and now embodied in legal decisions.

Condition Term which is vital to a contract. Breach of a condition destroys the basis of the contract which is itself then breached.

Consideration Consists either in some right, interest, profit or benefit accruing to one party contract, or some forbearance, detriment, loss or responsibility given, suffered or undertaken by the other.

Constructive dismissal Serious breach of contract by an employer which forces an employee to leave.

Consumer Any natural person who, in contracts covered by the regulations, is acting outside his trade, business as progression.

Contract An agreement which legally binds the parties.

Contract of employment A contract of employment is 'a contract of service or apprenticeship, whether express or implied, and (if it is express) whether it is oral or in writing.'

Control test Test used by the courts to determine whether a contract of employment exists, or whether a party is an independent contractor.

Damages The sum claimed or awarded in a civil action in compensation for the loss or injury suffered by the claimant.

Decision A source of European law, which may be addressed to a state, person or a company and is immediately binding, but only on the recipient.

Defendant The person against whom a civil action is brought or who is prosecuted for a criminal offence.

Delegated legislation Rules of law made by subordinate bodies to whom the power to do so has been given by statute.

Directive A term of European Community law, issued to the government of the EU states requiring them within a certain specified period (usually two years) to alter the national laws of the state so that they conform to the directive.

Dismissal Termination by an employer of a contract of employment.

Enforceable code of practice A code of practice that is enforceable by means of sanctions falling short of legal proceedings. It will set down codes of conduct that can be enforced against people engaged in a certain trade or business, even though they are not members of the relevant trade body.

Equity A source of English law consisting of those rules which emerged from the Court of Chancery.

Estoppel When a person, by his words or conduct, leads another to believe that a certain state of affairs exists. If the other person alters his or her position to his or her detriment in reliance on that belief, the first person is estopped (prevented) from claiming later that a different state of affairs existed.

Exclusion clause Contract clause purporting to exclude or restrict liability.

Executed consideration A performed, or executed, act in return for a promise.

Executory consideration A promise given for a promise, not a performed act.

Force majeure clauses Clauses inserted in contracts when the parties can foresee that difficulties are likely to arise but the parties cannot foresee their precise nature of extent.

Fundamental breach Doctrine developed by the courts as a protection against unreasonable exemption clauses in contracts.

Implied term Term deemed to form part of a contract even though not expressly mentioned by the parties.

In personam An action *in personam* is one seeking relief against a particular person.

In rem An action *in rem* is one brought in respect of property.

Independent contractor Self-employed person.

Indictable offences Are serious offences that can only be heard in a Crown court.

Injunction An equitable remedy in which the court orders the other party to a contract to observe negative restrictions.

Integration test Test used by the courts to determine whether a contract of employment exists.

Intention to create legal relations Element necessary for an agreement to become a legally binding contract.

Invitation to treat Indication that someone is prepared to receive offers with a view to forming a binding contract. It is not on offer in itself.

Lien A right to retain possession of property until a debt has been paid.

Minor A person under the age of eighteen.

Misrepresentation False statement made with the object of inducing the other party to enter into a contract.

Multiple test Used by the courts to determine whether a contract of employment exists.

Obiter dicta Statements made by a judge 'by the way'.

Offer A definate promise to be bound on specific terms.

Office of Fair Trading A government department staffed by over 300 people and financed by the Department of Trade and Industry. It is headed by the Director General of Fair Trading (DGFT), supported by a Deputy Director General. It does not usually deal with complaints received directly from members of the general public, but acts on information from the following sources:

(a)   Its own investigations
(b)   Information provided by local authority trading standards departments
(c)   The courts (who inform the DGFT of material convictions)
(d)   News media

Ombudsman Used to describe the provision of a final independent appeal that a dissatisfied customer may make against what he or she believes to be unfair or incompetent treatment. (The term is Swedish and does not have a satisfactory English translation.) Some Ombudsmen are provided with government support. In the private sector, banks, building societies and insurance companies may support Ombudsmen on a voluntary basis.

Past consideration Something already done at the time that a contractual promise is made.

Penalty clause In a contract providing for a specific sum to be payable in the event of a subsequent breach.

Per se By itself.

Persons at work Anyone who comes within the scope of the employer while undertaking their own work. This therefore would include employees, independent contractors, visitors who are visiting for business purposes (for example, suppliers or professional advisers).

Persons other than persons at work appears to mean any persons, extending to the general public.

Precedent A previous court decision.

Privity of contract The relation between two parties to a contract.

Quantum meruit As much as he has deserved.

Ratio decidendi The reason for the decision.

Re In the matter of. Seen in some case names.

Rectification An equitable remedy in which the court can order a document to be altered so that it reflects the parties true intentions.

Regulation A form of European Community law which became part of the law of each member nation as soon as they come into force without the need for each country to make its own legislation.

Remoteness of damage Relationship between a wrongful act and the resulting damage which determines whether or not compensation may be recovered. Different principles apply in contract and in tort.

Rescission An equitable remedy through which a contract is cancelled or rejected and the parties are restored to their pre-contracted position, as if it had never been entered into.

Royal Assent Final stage in the process by which a Bill becomes an Act.

Sale of goods A contract whereby the seller transfers or agrees to transfer the property in goods for a money consideration called the price.

Seller/supplier Any natural or legal person who, in contracts covered by the regulations, is acting for the purposes relating to his trade, business or profession, whether publicly owned or privately owned.

Specific performance An equitable remedy in which the court orders the defendant to perform his side of a contract.

Standard form contract A standard document prepared by many large organisations and setting out the terms on which they contract with their customers.

Standard of proof The extent to which the court must be satisfied by the evidence presented.

Statutory instrument Form of delegated legislation.

Summary offences Are minor crimes, only triable summarily in magistrates' courts.

Uberrimae fidei Of utmost good faith.

Ultra vires Beyond their powers. In company law this term is used in connection with transactions which are outside the scope of the objects clause and therefore, in principle at least, unenforceable. In an *ultra vires* contract the company would not have had the capacity to contract.

Unenforceable contract Is a valid contract and property transferred under it cannot be recovered even from the other party to the contract if either party refuses to perform the contract, the other party cannot compel him to do so

Void contract Not a contract at all. The parties are not bound by it and if they transfer property under it they can sometimes recover their goods from a third party.

Voidable contract A contract which one party may avoid, that is, terminate at his option. Property transferred before avoidance is usually irrecoverable from a third party.

Warranty Minor term in a contract. It does not go to the root of the contract, but is subsidiary to the main purpose of the contract. Breach of a warranty does not give rise to breach of the contract itself.

TABLE OF CASES

NOTES

INDEX

NOTES

NOTES

BPP
PROFESSIONAL EDUCATION

See overleaf for information on other
BPP products and how to order

HND/HNC Order

To BPP Professional Education, Aldine Place, London W12 8AW
Tel: 020 8740 2211. Fax: 020 8740 1184
E-mail: Publishing@bpp.com Web:www.bpp.com

Mr/Mrs/Ms (Full name)
Daytime delivery address

Postcode

Daytime Tel   E-mail

5/04

Course Books

MANDATORY (£9.95 each)

Unit 1 Marketing ☐
Unit 2 Managing Financial Resources and Decisions ☐
Unit 3 Organisations and Behaviour ☐
Unit 4 Business Environment ☐
Unit 5 Common Law I ☐
Unit 6 Business Decision Making ☐
Unit 7 Business Strategy ☐
Unit 8 Research Project ☐

Special offer: Buy all 8 Mandatory Texts for £70 ☐

ENDORSED TITLE ROUTES (£14.95 each)

Units 9-12 Finance ☐
Units 13-16 Management ☐
Units 17-20 Marketing ☐
Units 21-24 Human Resource Management ☐
Units 25-28 Law ☐

Special offer: Buy any 2 Endorsed Title Routes for £25 ☐

SUBTOTAL £ ☐

TOTAL FOR PRODUCTS £ ☐

POSTAGE & PACKING

Texts	First	Each extra	Online
UK	£5.00	£2.00	£2.00 £
Europe*	£6.00	£4.00	£4.00 £
Rest of world	£20.00	£10.00	£10.00 £

TOTAL FOR POSTAGE & PACKING £ ☐

Grand Total (Cheques to *BPP Professional Education*)

I enclose a cheque for (incl. Postage) £ ☐
Or charge to Access/Visa/Switch
Card Number ☐☐☐☐ ☐☐☐☐ ☐☐☐☐ ☐☐☐☐   CV2 No ☐☐☐
last 3 digits on signature strip

Expiry date ☐☐☐☐   Start Date ☐☐☐☐

Issue Number (Switch Only) ☐☐

Signature

We aim to deliver to all UK addresses inside 5 working days; a signature will be required. Orders to all EU addresses should be delivered within 6 working days. All other orders to overseas addresses should be delivered within 8 working days. * Europe includes the Republic of Ireland and the Channel Islands.

Review Form & Free Prize Draw – HND Mandatory Unit 5 – Common Law I (6/04)

All original review forms from the entire BPP range, completed with genuine comments, will be entered into one of two draws on 31 January 2005 and 31 July 2005. The names on the first four forms picked out on each occasion will be sent a cheque for £50.

Name: _____   Address: _____

_____

_____

How have you used this Course Book?
(Tick one box only)

☐ Home study (book only)

☐ On a course: college _____

☐ Other _____

Why did you decide to purchase this Course book? *(Tick one box only)*

☐ Have used BPP Texts in the past

☐ Recommendation by friend/colleague

☐ Recommendation by a lecturer at college

☐ Saw advertising

☐ Other _____

During the past six months do you recall seeing/receiving any of the following?
(Tick as many boxes as are relevant)

☐ Our advertisement

☐ Our brochure with a letter through the post

Your ratings, comments and suggestions would be appreciated on the following areas

	Very useful	Useful	Not useful
Introductory pages	☐	☐	☐
Topic coverage	☐	☐	☐
Summary diagrams	☐	☐	☐
Chapter roundups	☐	☐	☐
Quick quizzes	☐	☐	☐
Activities	☐	☐	☐
Discussion points	☐	☐	☐

	Excellent	Good	Adequate	Poor
Overall opinion of this Course book	☐	☐	☐	☐

Do you intend to continue using BPP HND/HNC Course books?   ☐ Yes   ☐ No

Please note any further comments and suggestions/errors on the reverse of this page.

The BPP author of this edition can be e-mailed at: pippariley@bpp.com

Please return this form to: Pippa Riley, BPP Professional Education, FREEPOST, London, W12 8BR

Review Form & Free Prize Draw (continued)

Please note any further comments and suggestions/errors below

Free Prize Draw Rules

1   Closing date for 31 January 2005 draw is 31 December 2004. Closing date for 31 July 2005 draw is 30 June 2005.

2   Restricted to entries with UK and Eire addresses only. BPP employees, their families and business associates are excluded.

3   No purchase necessary. Entry forms are available upon request from BPP Professional Education. No more than one entry per title, per person. Draw restricted to persons aged 16 and over.

4   Winners will be notified by post and receive their cheques not later than 6 weeks after the relevant draw date.

5   The decision of the promoter in all matters is final and binding. No correspondence will be entered into.